MASTERS OR SLAVES?

'This book shines brightly in the constellation of books on the subject. Written by an expert, it is historically situated, technologically informed, well modulated in tone, coherent in argument, theological in orientation, and judicious in illustrations. More than a book of conclusions, its design and structure model the best in the art of robust critique while offering possible ways to consider the appropriate deployment of artificial intelligence.'
Bruce A. Little PhD, Professor Emeritus of Philosophy, Southeastern Baptist Theological Seminary, USA

MASTERS OR SLAVES?

AI and the future of humanity

Jeremy Peckham

ivp

INTER-VARSITY PRESS
36 Causton Street, London SW1P 4ST, England
Email: ivp@ivpbooks.com
Website: www.ivpbooks.com

First published 2021

British Library Cataloguing-in-Publication Data
A catalogue record for this book is available from the British Library.

ISBN: 978–1–78974–239–8
eBook ISBN: 978–1–78974–240–4

Set in 11/14pt Minion Pro
Typeset in Great Britain by CRB Associates, Potterhanworth, Lincolnshire
Printed and bound in Great Britain by Ashford Colour Press Ltd, Gosport, Hampshire

Produced on paper from sustainable forests.

Inter-Varsity Press publishes Christian books that are true to the Bible and that communicate the gospel, develop discipleship and strengthen the church for its mission in the world.

IVP originated within the Inter-Varsity Fellowship, now the Universities and Colleges Christian Fellowship, a student movement connecting Christian Unions in universities and colleges throughout Great Britain, and a member movement of the International Fellowship of Evangelical Students. Website: www.uccf.org.uk. That historic association is maintained, and all senior IVP staff and committee members subscribe to the UCCF Basis of Faith.

To

Miriam, Livia, Rafe, Lucas, Rueben, Jackson, William and Sophia, my delightful grandchildren who bring such joy, with the prayer that they and their generation will be masters of their digital world.

Contents

Preface

The genesis of this book goes back to a conversation I overheard at the breakfast table between Professor Bruce Little and a group of PhD students. Bruce commented that there were two key areas that he thought Christians needed to be taking seriously and thinking about today, AI (artificial intelligence) and neuroscience. That comment piqued my interest as AI was an area in which I had spent much of my career.

When I started out in the research and development of computer speech and language understanding systems, it was not fashionable to refer to such work as AI. My research at the Royal Aircraft Establishment was on whether speech input to computers could lessen the burden on fighter pilots, whose routine tasks, along with flying a sophisticated aircraft, required manual data entry to update on-board systems, such as navigation aids. This seemed like a beneficial use of what's now routinely called AI: assisting a pilot to carry out complex tasks and reducing stress.

When I entered the commercial world and became involved in developing computer-based speech understanding systems for use over the telephone, I had little thought for the ethical implications of its use, except perhaps in so far as it might have displaced some call-centre workers. Even then the thought was that such technology would increase capacity, rather than serve as a direct replacement of human agents. Speech recognition systems were also seen as a way to allow safe use of mobile phones when driving.

Fast forward to today and we can now talk to our smartphones and digital agents at our bank and shop online without touching a keyboard. Algorithms, similar to those that have so successfully been used to recognize what you say to your smartphone, have found their way into a host of other applications, such as facial recognition, self-drive vehicles and drug discovery.

Following Bruce's comment, I began thinking more deeply about the ethical issues surrounding AI. What's it about this technology that inspires technologists, yet at the same time creates so much fear when we see it used in mass surveillance or to replace workers?

As my ideas began to come together, I was invited to present a series of talks over a couple of days to the International Fellowship of Evangelical Students Graduate Impact science and politics groups. It was not long after giving those talks that I participated in a round-table discussion on AI ethics, initiated by a well-known advocacy organization. I was surprised to find that there were differences of views around the table on the ethical implications of a variety of AI applications, from self-drive vehicles to sex robots. For me the issues centred around whether some uses of AI could diminish our ability to mirror God's image in us. Some involved in the discussion couldn't see why it might be wrong to allow artefacts, such as self-drive vehicles, to have full autonomy or even for sex robots to have rights, in order to protect humans from abusing them.

That discussion was the impetus to flesh out and put in writing the thoughts that I had been developing around the potential dangers to humanity of some deployments of AI in our world today. Grounded in my understanding of what the Bible teaches about humanity, made in the image of God, and our responsibility to be image bearers, outlined in chapter 4, I developed a taxonomy of AI applications. This taxonomy is presented in chapter 11 and forms the backbone of my thinking about how humanity is being shaped by AI and, more widely, digital technology.

My concerns in this book are more about the threats already posed by today's capabilities, rather than some dystopian future with superintelligent robots controlling the world. As I write these words, we're in the midst of a pandemic that has brought unprecedented controls on movement and association, to protect our lives and avoid overburdening our health services. The deployment of so-called intelligent robots to avoid humans being put at risk has accelerated. Many nations are rolling out smartphone applications to track whether people have been in contact with someone who has tested positive for Covid-19. Poland, in an alarmingly dystopian scenario to enforce quarantine using facial recognition, requires people to upload a selfie from their smartphone application within twenty minutes of an alert, or the police are dispatched to their home. As with so many ethical issues, the danger is that one justification for stepping over a boundary leads to another. Over time we become desensitized to the original issue and it's thereby normalized in our society.

I've set out in this book to alert the reader to a number of specific threats to our humanness, as judged against what the Bible teaches about being made in God's image and our calling to be faithful image bearers. It's my hope that you'll be stimulated to think further, dig into the Bible, discuss the issues with others and, where necessary, take action, in order that we may be masters of this technology, rather than become unwitting slaves to it.

Jeremy Peckham

Acknowledgments

I am grateful to Bruce Little, Professor Emeritus of Philosophy at Southeastern Baptist Theological Seminary in the USA, who first sparked my interest in the ethical issues surrounding AI. He and I have engaged in many discussions on the topic of AI and his numerous comments on my early draft were most helpful. In particular Bruce introduced me to the key questions that we need to ask – what does this technology do *for* us and what does it do *to* us, what's gained and what's lost? These questions were seminal in my arriving at the conclusions that I have in this book, addressed in the context of what I understand to be the Bible's teaching about the nature of humanity.

Thanks are also due to Martin Yates, who inspired me to write the narrative introduction to the book in the prologue as well as the short story in chapter 5; his stylistic suggestions were invaluable. My intentions were to create a slightly edgy but realistic overview of the challenges of AI today. Any failures in that regard are entirely my responsibility.

I would also like to thank Philip Duce, Senior Commissioning Editor at Inter-Varsity Press, whose scrutiny of my early manuscript prompted a rewrite that, in my opinion at least, has resulted in a far better presentation of the material. Copy editor Eldo Barkhuizen did a splendid job, tirelessly editing the manuscript, spotting inconsistencies and carefully checking each reference. This work would not have been possible without the support of my dear wife, Jan, who has long been a sounding board for my ideas and an insightful companion in theological discussion. Her patience and encouragement through long hours of research, writing and rewriting have helped me to produce the work that you now have in your hands.

1
Prologue

The dawning of a new day?

The alarm on Matt's smartphone grows louder and louder as he gradually emerges from sleep into the awareness of a new day dawning. It's still dark outside, but Matt's mind has already begun fussing about what lies ahead. He stretches over to turn off the alarm and, conscious that Katie is probably still asleep, whispers, 'Alexa, what's the weather going to be like today?'

'Foggy all day and cold,' comes the softly whispered, somewhat conspiratorial, reply from the white doughnut-sized disc on the bedside table as it pulses with a soft blue light.

Katie stirs and groans, 'Oh, not another miserable day.' January seems to have been going on for ever, and now she's remembering that this morning she has to trek across the city to one of the other distribution centres where they're commissioning a new picking system. She feels an actual pain in the pit of her stomach as she realizes that today is the day that she must make about half of the workforce redundant. She worries about whether they'll find other work despite attempts made at upgrading and reskilling those affected. Most of them just hadn't really taken to programming or even seemed that interested. Katie turns over and pulls the duvet up a little tighter.

'I didn't mean to disturb you,' Matt says, stretching and yawning.

'It's OK: I was already disturbed,' Katie mumbles. 'Thinking about the commissioning, the redundancies and all that, you know.' She turns back over towards Matt. 'And Alexa's voice is pretty disturbing when she whispers. I can't quite get used to the idea that she – it – knows when you lower your voice and seems to understand how you might be feeling. It's a bit creepy – like having another woman in our bedroom.'

'I think maybe you're just a bit oversensitive this morning,' Matt replies briskly, as he swings his legs out of bed, sits up and slides his feet into his slippers. 'Alexa, what's the news?' he asks just as briskly, not whispering any more.

After a moment's pause, Alexa's soft feminine voice begins, 'China has signed an agreement for another consignment of weaponized drones to the Indian government. Meanwhile, talks are still continuing with government representatives from over fifty nations over the banning of lethal autonomous weapons.'

'Fat chance that will have of succeeding,' Katie mutters on her way to check if the children are up.

'Why's that?' Matt asks, heading to the bathroom, so that he finishes while Katie organizes the children.

'There are too many vested interests,' she calls after him as she heads for the children's rooms.

'Yeah, but maybe this is the future of warfare. Surely, autonomous weapons will help to keep humans out of direct conflict.'

'Yeah, that's all very well, but are you happy to let AI decide who is targeted and if the target is genuine?' Katie calls after him, as he disappears into the bathroom, and she opens her 8-year-old's bedroom door. Joe is lying on his bed talking to the WonderBot that he got for Christmas.

'Hi Joe, it's time to get dressed and have some breakfast,' says Katie in a bright voice. She makes her way over to the bed, picking up toys already strewn across the floor from Joe's early morning play.

'Don't want to,' intones Joe as he sits up, cuddling his robot in his arms. 'I'm talking to Owly.'

'Owly?' Katie asks.

'Yes, his name's Owly now,' the 8-year-old replies matter-of-factly, 'because he looks like the owl we saw down the lane by the farm.'

'OK.' Katie isn't convinced by the likeness, apart from the eyes perhaps, but there are bigger things to deal with right now. 'Come on, Joey, you've got to get ready or you'll be late for your lift to school and you'll miss Charlie.'

'We don't care about Charlie any more,' Joe whines, 'do we, Owly? He's boring.'

Owly whirrs and bleeps a few times, and then announces, 'Charlie is boring.'

Katie wonders whether buying the toy robot for his eighth birthday was such a good idea after all. And the idea of linking it up to Alexa seems like a bad move.

Katie looks across sternly at Joe. 'Don't be so rude about Charlie. He's your best friend. Now, up and dressed and downstairs in the next ten minutes. Got it?'

As she leaves the room, Katie realizes that she subconsciously addressed her comments to Joe *and* Owly.

On the door across the landing the new home-made sign has a selfie of a defiant-looking 13-year-old and in a space-age neon-pink font the words '*ELLIE'S DOMAIN. KNOCK AND WAIT*'. Through the crack in the door, Katie sees the glow of her daughter's smartphone. She was on it till late last night, and who knows how long she's been on it already this morning – doing whatever and chatting to whomever? Katie sometimes shudders to think . . .

'What d'you want?' comes the voice from within. 'I know you're snooping by the door.'

'Time to be getting up for school, love,' Katie says in the cheeriest most non-confrontational voice possible. Right now, the diplomacy involved in making a hundred employees redundant seems pretty straightforward.

'I'm doing my geography homework. I'll come down when I've finished,' comes the impatient reply. 'I don't want breakfast anyway.'

Katie decides, wisely or otherwise, that she's going in. As she does so, she catches the canned voice of her daughter's phone announcing that there are two presidents of Venezuela.

'That doesn't sound right,' Katie remarks as she ventures awkwardly into her daughter's domain. A thought is coming to her that Venezuela had a disputed election that hadn't really been resolved. 'I don't think they do actually have two presidents.'

'It's what Alexa says,' retorts Ellie.

Katie can't hold in a snort of derision.

Ellie reacts to it, sharply. 'Well, she knows far more than you or Dad – and I'm in a rush – it's due in today – you know what Miss Jackson's like.'

'But shouldn't you just check it out, Ellie? Maybe look at a few history or news sites to be sure?' says Katie.

'I don't have time!' Ellie snaps. 'And anyway, why would Alexa say that if it wasn't true? They must have two presidents for some reason. They wouldn't let her give out wrong answers, would they?'

Katie realizes the question is rhetorical and the last thing she wants this morning is a fight with Ellie about the politics of Venezuela.

'OK,' she says. 'I just don't want you relying on Alexa for everything. You should think for yourself. Check your facts.' Ellie is making a show of yawning, so Katie changes tack. 'Are you OK getting the bus this morning? I have to drive over to the other side of town to one of our warehouses. Tell a hundred people that they don't have a job any more because machines can do their job quicker and cheaper.'

'Sure, whatever,' Ellie says, distracted by a ping on her smartphone. The irony is lost on her.

Katie, worrying about Ellie, heads to the bathroom. She and Matt really must make time to sit down and talk about how much time Ellie is spending on her phone and tablet, and on that virtual reality (VR) game that she bought with her Christmas money. It's as if, with or without those VR glasses on, she's in another world. Katie's sure that Ellie is more introverted and impatient now than she was even a year ago, and it hits her that she hasn't experienced anything other than this permanently switched-on, hi-tech world. And Joe too. He's only 8 and it's already affecting him.

It's all so different from when she and Matt were children.

Katie brushes past Matt, who is standing in front of the bathroom mirror brushing his teeth with the tap full on.

'You're wasting water,' she tells him as she steps into the shower cubicle. 'Turn it off while you're brushing.'

'What?'

Matt is deep in thought, wondering who to hire for the new user-interface-design role from the shortlist of candidates he met yesterday. He's sorry to be losing Sue, who's been offered a senior position by one of their competitors at a salary he can't match. Besides, they don't really have an opening for a more senior position at the moment. So he can understand why she's moving on.

Still, he muses, she was so shy and reserved when they took her on but she had such a great CV and a First from Cambridge. She'd turned out to be really dedicated and was quite easy to get on with, once you got to know her. He thinks about Josh, one of the candidates shortlisted by HireCheck, the new software package that HR (Human Resources) has just started to use to screen job applicants. He seems just a bit larger than life and Matt wonders if Josh has been able to fake it in HireCheck's selection process.

Matt has been told that the system is very clever and able to measure candidates' emotion from their voice and facial expressions. He wonders if the system could be manipulated, but quickly dismisses the idea. Nevertheless, he's pretty sure that HireCheck would never have picked Sue, yet she's proved to be great for the company and a superb colleague. However, he may come across as a Luddite if he questions the new technology. His final spit into the basin has some blood in it. He watches it spiral down the plughole and hopes everything will be all right.

'Shut the door!' Katie yells from the shower as he shuffles back to the bedroom to get dressed.

Fifteen minutes later, everyone is in the kitchen. Even Ellie, who has compromised with a cereal bar. She now has her earbuds in and is catching up on various social media platforms at the same time. Katie is scrolling through Facebook and Matt is checking last night's midweek football matches. The only conversation is between Joe and Owly, who are still discussing their dislike of Charlie and a few other ex-friends in Year 2.

Putting his phone down, Matt decides to pursue the previous line of argument. 'So don't you think autonomous weapons might depersonalize war? Take some of the loss of human life out of it?'

'Like a big game of World of Warcraft?' Katie suggests ironically, clearing Joe's bowl away and wiping the breakfast bar.

'Yeah,' Matt replies, missing the irony completely. 'I guess so.'

'I was joking,' Katie says dismissively. 'Don't you think it's a bit scary having all those autonomous weapons out there, like a crazy game, not knowing what nutcase is in control, and how they decide whom to target, or whether they could be hacked by an even bigger nutcase?'

'No more so than having our roads full of self-driving cars and delivery trucks,' Matt replies.

'Yeah, that's an issue too,' Katie agrees. 'They're not quite the same as weapons but you're still handing over life-and-death choices to a machine; they could still kill . . .'

'But not deliberately, surely?'

Katie just raises her eyebrows and gives Matt a look that shows she's not as sure as he is. Then she breaks off and grabs Joe's coat and book bag. 'Come on, Joey. It's time to go. Say goodbye to Dad and Ellie . . . and Owly.'

'Owly says he wants to come to school,' Joe says in a tone that shows he knows it's not going to happen.

'WonderBots are too clever for school,' Matt interjects. 'They know everything already.'

'Matt, don't encourage that myth. We'll talk later.'

With that, Katie is whisking the 8-year-old out of the door. 'Come on, little man. Owly will still be here when you get home. Time to go and mix with some real children.'

'Ellie, don't miss the bus!' she calls loudly.

'It's OK. I've got ages,' Ellie replies nonchalantly, removing one earbud. 'Ryan says his mum will pick me up on the way past.'

'Ryan?'

'Yeah, we chat online all the time,' she shrugs, popping the earbud back in. 'He's in Year 10. Thinks I'm cute.'

'Maybe we'll talk about Ryan later,' Katie says, not even sure she can be heard.

'Hope the warehouse visit isn't too stressful,' Matt says, as he gives Katie a quick kiss and pecks Joe on the forehead as he's scrambled out of the back door to the waiting car. 'Don't worry, buddy. I'll sit Owly on the sofa so he can learn new stuff from the TV all day. He doesn't even need it switched on.'

Katie drops Joe off at Anita's – she's Charlie's mum and will take both of the boys to school in about half an hour. Katie wonders if she should warn Anita about the business with Owly, just in case Joe says something that upsets Charlie, but decides against it – it'll all probably sound a bit weird and over-sensitive.

As Katie heads west across the city the day is as grey and miserable as Alexa promised. Katie takes the bypass that goes the long way round, but will enable her to get to the warehouse without going through the worst of the traffic. It's so much quicker now that they've finished the smart-city network and upgraded the cameras. As she joins the bypass, she notices that the cameras are spaced every 100 metres apart.

Despite her reservations, Katie can't help loving how much more efficient things are nowadays. With smart cities and efficient transport systems, and security cameras, and global connectivity, and Alexa in every room to switch on the lights, turn up the heating, get the latest news, etcetera, etcetera.

As she drifts westwards through the cold grey morning, in her warm, air-conditioned, humidity-controlled car, she wonders where it's all going. Her own life and Matt's are so much more convenient than the life their parents must've experienced. But never mind the past. What about the future for all the workers that she'll have to lay off today – and so many others like them all over the world? AI has taken off like an express train, and everyone keeps saying how much more convenient it is to talk to computers and have machines make decisions for us.

And what about Ellie and Joe and all the other children who seem so caught up in all this tech that controls their lives and everything they think and say and do? The trouble is, everyone's caught up in it – not just youngsters – and it's hard to break out of. And is anyone really any happier for all of this? Maybe, because there are advantages too of course.

The smart city can track her every movement and someone can know where she, Katie Jefferson, is at any moment. What shops she visits and maybe even what she's bought there. They know that anyway, she thinks, because everything she buys is stored and processed to help her have a 'better shopping experience' as Matt always puts it when they discuss it together. They often debate whether the state and Big Tech are getting too cosy, sharing people's data.

As she approaches the Westside industrial estate, Katie glances up at the cameras pointing at her and the surrounding street and is grateful that the police were able to foil a potential break-in last week when the cameras did their job. Yet she has mixed feelings about the links between the estate's security cameras and the smart-city system that tracks people's movements, remembers their locations, knows who they are with. The move to 'smart policing' still worries her on many levels. But it must make for a safer world, surely.

Katie is still thinking hard as she turns into the industrial estate and approaches the distribution warehouse – a huge silver edifice that shimmers a little in the cold January light, a monument to progress. Katie parks her car in one of the spaces reserved for management. A drone hovers over the car park. She's not sure why. The media probably. She wonders just how safe she really feels.

Leaving the cosy controlled environment of her car for the cold grey of this bleak day, Katie shivers as she makes her way towards the main entrance. Her mind is turning to the improved profits and efficiency that will result from her company fully automating their warehouse. She still has a nagging concern as she contemplates the uncertain future of the workers who will lose their jobs today. And how long will it be before management roles suffer the same fate?

Katie enters the fully automated security checking system where she'll be scanned. No need for embarrassment any more – her scan will be processed automatically. Yet no longer will she share the normal pleasantries with Jim, who used to man security. He was made redundant six months ago. She wonders about him, his wife and family.

Katie braces herself for the next few hours when she'll speak to each worker being laid off. Making her way down management row, she sees a ghost, catches a glimpse of her own reflection in one of the glass walls. 'What's happening to us?' she wonders. 'Profits and productivity are up. We're winning a bigger share of the global market, but at what cost? Are we gaining the world but losing our souls?'

Today's realities

The issues that face the Jefferson family in the first few hours of their day aren't set in some dystopian future but are today's realities as far as the deployment of AI, machine learning and intelligent robotics is concerned. They raise urgent questions for anyone concerned about the future of humanity and our part in an increasingly automated and connected hi-tech world.

What exactly is the right balance between efficiency and a loss of the old way of doing things, ways that meant getting along with people, building relationships face to face, caring for our families and elderly parents? Will we be able to retrain workers and create new jobs to replace those lost by the march of automation? Does it matter whether we or a machine makes moral choices if some lives may be saved, or if a better decision can be made?

My aim in this book is to help us answer some of these questions and explore whether applications of AI can really harm us and, if so, in what ways. We begin in chapter 2 with an overview of what AI technology is, what can be achieved and what may be possible in the future.

Many consider technology to be a neutral entity: it has no moral bias. Rather, it's what we as humans do with it that matters. We examine this view in chapter 3 and find that it's not a true reflection of the reality of our day-to-day dealings with technology, whether it be our smartphone or a sophisticated piece of AI software for screening job candidates. The chapter concludes by considering how the Enlightenment has shaped our view of progress and technology's role in that.

Regardless of our view of technology per se, we cannot know whether we're being shaped in a good or bad way unless we first understand what it means to be human. A Christian anthropology is located in the Bible and we'll explore this in chapter 4, discovering what it has to teach us about ourselves, and in particular what it means to be made after God's likeness.

The questions that arose in Matt and Katie's minds revolved around several different ways in which AI technologies are having an impact on humanity, from the effects of job loss on unskilled workers to digital assistants, such as Alexa and toy robots, on our children's relationships. I've identified six ways in which our humanness is influenced, and each of these is elaborated in some detail in chapters 5–10. Where it exists, I've sought to provide empirical evidence for the specific influences on humanity, and to show how these may conflict with a biblical understanding of what it means to be human, discussed in chapter 4.

We begin our journey in chapter 5, where we explore how AI is influencing our cognitive abilities and skills in the workplace, as AI learns them, competes with us and eventually wins, as it did in the AlphaGo game competing with Lee Sedol, the world champion.

In chapter 6 we'll look at how simulations of humanlike behaviour are taking us away from developing real relationships and are creating attachments to things, even to the point of feeling that we owe them an ethical obligation and that they ought to have rights.

Chapter 7 considers the impact that AI is having on our privacy and freedom, with the internet of things (IoT), smart cities and mass surveillance by facial recognition technology. In this chapter we'll also discover the increasing impact that Big Tech is having on our privacy and freedom as more and more of our data gets sucked up, processed by AI and sold to advertisers.

In chapter 8 we'll explore how our role as vicegerents, our moral accountability and our responsibility to God determines how we should view self-drive vehicles and autonomous weapons when they take on moral agency.

We return to the impact of AI on our workplace in chapter 9 by looking at the threat to the jobs of both blue- and white-collar workers. Finally, in chapter 10 we consider whether engaging with virtual and augmented reality could cause us to lose reality altogether.

Chapter 11 draws together the threads of the preceding arguments and presents a framework for us to use to evaluate the potential influences of AI applications. Some practical guidelines are offered to enable us to determine what to do about these influences. A virtue approach to resolving ethical tensions in the deployment of AI applications is proposed, rather than defaulting to the criterion of convenience.

Chapter 12 draws the book to a conclusion with a Christian manifesto for AI and some conclusions for us as individuals, churches and wider society. The chapter provides a brief review of what various official bodies around the world are doing to address the concerns raised in the book. I end with a final challenge to us all, to follow the true *Homo Deus* and not compromise our ability to be imitators of Christ.

2
Artificially intelligent

The term 'artificial intelligence' (AI) was coined by computer scientist John McCarthy early in his career in 1955, as the title for a conference aimed at exploring ways in which a machine could reason like a human. He defined the term as 'the science and engineering of making intelligent machines'.[1] He believed that 'every aspect of learning or any other feature of intelligence can, in principle be so precisely described that a machine can be made to simulate it'.[2] Decades later AI is everywhere and being applied to a vast array of applications from assessing the likelihood of petty criminals reoffending to identifying cancer tumours.

When the famous chess victory was won by IBM's Deep Blue computer in 1997 against the reigning world champion Garry Kasparov, many thought this to be the dawn of AI. It can be argued that Deep Blue wasn't really artificial intelligence at all but a brute force approach to working out all the possible moves in chess up to several moves ahead, following the human player's moves. It was capable of calculating 200 million positions per second – clearly something beyond human capability.

The basis for early AI technology, long before the chess victory, was to try to encode the rules governing human decision-making, in order for a computer to emulate the thinking that a human goes through in problem solving. Such systems became known

1 J. McCarthy, *What Is Artificial Intelligence?* (Stanford, Calif.: Computer Science Department, Stanford University, 2007), p. 2, retrieved on 11 September 2020 from <http://jmc.stanford.edu/articles/whatisai/whatisai.pdf>.

2 McCarthy, M. I. Minsky, N. Rochester and C. E. Shannon, 'A Proposal for the Dartmouth Summer Research Project on Artificial Intelligence' (unpublished manuscript held in Stanford University archives, 31 August 1955), reproduced in *AI Magazine* 27 (4) (2006), p. 12.

as 'expert systems' and even today are referred to as 'traditional AI'. However, these early expert systems and the claims made for AI using this approach failed to produce anything remarkable in terms of simulating human capability. Nor did they result in any useful applications.

What is intelligence anyway?

In 1950, prior to McCarthy's coining the term 'artificial intelligence', British scientist Alan Turing published his seminal paper 'Computer Machinery and Intelligence'. In it he described a test that could be used to determine whether a machine can think. The test was based on the party game where a man and a woman go into separate rooms and guests try to tell them apart. This is done by guests writing a series of questions to them and looking at their written answers.

Instead of having two humans in separate rooms, the idea of the Turing test is that one is a human and the other a computer. An interrogator must determine which is which by asking a series of written questions and considering the written responses. If the interrogator judges the computer to be a human, then it can be deemed to be 'thinking'. This test has been widely criticized as too simplistic and much debate continues today in the philosophy of artificial intelligence as to what really constitutes human intelligence or, more precisely, the ability to think.

In 1966 Joseph Weizenbaum developed a program called ELIZA that seemed to pass Turing's test using keyword spotting from the written sentences supplied and responding using a set of rules to produce replies. If no keyword was found, the program responded with a repost or by repeating an earlier comment. Some people were fooled into thinking that they were talking to a real person. Chatbots in use today frequently fool people into thinking that they're speaking with a person.

Philosopher John Searle argued in a paper 'Minds, Brains and Programs' in 1980 that the Turing test was an inadequate test for whether a computer could think, since it was simply responding to a set of symbols, without any understanding, and was not thinking at all. He proposed the 'Chinese room' thought experiment that asks the question 'Does a computer that can take Chinese characters as input and respond appropriately literally understand Chinese or is it merely simulating the ability to understand Chinese?'[3] Searle suggested that if he were the person receiving the same characters, and had access to sufficient papers, pencils, erasers and filing cabinets, he could follow the program's instructions and produce Chinese characters as output, without understanding Chinese (which he doesn't) or understanding what the conversation was about.[4]

More recently Searle has suggested that consciousness is the ultimate target of the argument about a computer's ability to think. Turing foresaw this in his 1950 paper and said:

> I do not wish to give the impression that I think there is no mystery about consciousness. There is, for instance, something of a paradox connected with any attempt to localise it. But I do not think these mysteries necessarily need to be solved before we can answer the question with which we are concerned in this paper.[5]

Clearly, what Turing had in mind was the simulation of human ability, rather than suggesting that a computer could become conscious. These opposing arguments about whether a computer can or could ever think have become the foundation of heated discussions about what consciousness is or isn't and the philosophy of mind.

What's still clear today is that there's no widespread agreement as to what constitutes intelligence or consciousness, nor whether computers will be able to attain these human features. We'll return to this discussion in chapter 4 when we consider a Christian world

3 J. Searle, 'Minds, Brains and Programs', *Behavioral and Brain Sciences* 3 (3) (1980), pp. 417–424.
4 Ibid.
5 A. M. Turing, 'Computing Machinery and Intelligence', *Mind* 59 (236) (October 1950), p. 447.

view of true personhood and consciousness. For now we continue to explore the development of AI.

A winter of discontent!

The early development of expert systems in the 1960s through to the late 1970s failed to produce commercially useful programs and funding for research began to dry up. The field entered what has been called the 'AI winter'. During the early 1980s I was working for a multinational computer software company in the area of computer speech recognition. I first began working on this technology as a UK government scientist when the earliest machines were able only to recognize small vocabularies of words spoken one at a time, but only after the system had been trained to recognize a specific vocabulary. This was achieved by a user several times speaking each word in the required vocabulary. It was the start of the use of pattern recognition and was a break from the expert-system approach.

The computer didn't really care what the sound was that was spoken: its job was to analyse the spoken words and to store a pattern representing these words. The automatic recognition of spoken words was performed by pattern matching. This involved matching new input utterances with the stored patterns produced during the training session. We called this a sound-to-symbol transformation. Within the same laboratory where I worked, another division was experimenting with expert systems and new symbolic programming languages, such as LISP, invented by John McCarthy.

The problem with expert systems was that they required programmers to understand the rules surrounding a particular topic. An example might be how to pick company stocks that would be successful in the financial sector. Once the rules were understood, they were then encoded in a computer program. This was easier said than done!

The relative simplicity of matching patterns against pre-stored patterns seemed to achieve faster successes. The main drawback of this approach, whether for speech recognition, language translation or facial recognition, was its inability to generalize. The way we speak changes subtly between each utterance, even of the same word. Also, different speakers have different accents and, of course, we don't generally speak in monosyllables!

While we were able to develop computers that could recognize small vocabularies, such as numbers, they had no understanding of what those vocabularies meant, technically called semantics, nor of grammatical rules. In early speech-recognition systems these rules were encoded using the grammatical rules and meanings of words in each target language. This resulted in a hybrid of pattern matching and an expert system.

Breaking through

In the early 1980s we began developing statistically based algorithms called Hidden Markov Models, which were the forerunner of what is now called an artificial neural network (ANN). In computer-speech recognition these programs analysed lots of examples of spoken words from many different speakers. The result was a statistical representation of the variations that naturally occur in speech patterns.

When an utterance came to be recognized, the computer simply estimated how close a match it was to the stored statistical representation. The mathematics for this approach has been around since at least 1960 but required considerable computing power for real-world problems such as speech recognition. In order to achieve the computing power needed, the first version of a continuous-speech-recognition system, developed by my team in the 1980s and called Logos, required a large parallel array of computer chips.

This statistical approach to pattern recognition was a breakthrough because it was able to deal with the problem that no one utterance of the same word, spoken by the same person, is ever exactly the same. Furthermore, it enabled the technique to be generalized to recognize many different speakers, each speaking the same word, but with different accents. It also allowed the recognition of naturally spoken sentences, rather than requiring speakers to pause between each word in the sentence. When words are spoken in a continuous stream, the boundaries between each word become fuzzy, and the statistical technique can be extended to model the variations that occur when words are linked.

It was during this period that Geoffrey Hinton, then a professor at Carnegie Mellon University in the USA, co-invented Boltzmann Machines. They were a type of ANN that helped to popularize neural networks as an approach to machine learning. The idea of ANNs was conceived long before in the 1940s, and was inspired by the way in which biological nervous systems, such as the brain, process information.

Much is still unknown about how the brain trains itself and processes information, but the neurons in our brain appear to function as a highly interconnected network that collects and passes signals throughout that network. Neurons collect electrical signals through a network of fine structures called dendrites, and themselves send out signals through an axion that splits into thousands of branches. At the end of each branch the signals are modified by a synapse that inhibits or excites activity in the connected neurons.

An ANN mimics the function of the synapse by weighting the information passed from one 'neuron' to another with a threshold having to be reached to trigger that information being transferred. These weights and thresholds are learned during a training process, with the aim of optimizing the desired output (e.g. the picture presented to the computer is you) according to the labelled training data (e.g. lots of different pictures of you).

Although one strand of this research developed as a model for understanding the brain, another went on to use it as a means for solving problems in AI, such as image and speech recognition. So-called deep learning is simply an extension of the basic approach, but using multiple layers of ANNs to represent more features or information from presented training data. 'Deep learning' is a rather unfortunate term as it implies that the algorithms are somehow attaining deeper understanding. In fact, they're simply just more sophisticated pattern-matching algorithms.

Although the idea of ANNs was born in the 1940s and various developments ensued over the next few decades, the idea languished due to the significant computer power needed to carry out the necessary calculations for practical problems.

Fundamental to all neural network approaches is the requirement for significant amounts of data to train the algorithms or to 'learn' how to distinguish patterns, such as spoken sentences or images. Data is labelled as to what the desired output is, which may be recognizing that someone spoke my name, 'Jeremy', from multiple examples of people saying my name, referred to as training data. While there are a considerable number of different mathematical approaches to developing and training neural networks, they all tend to be variously described in general terms as 'machine learning', 'deep learning' or 'AI'. Although often confused with AI, machine learning is a subfield of AI, and ANNs form only a part of the suite of algorithms used in machine learning.

The algorithms that have been developed over the last few decades to simulate ANNs have become so good that they can now exceed the pattern-matching capabilities of humans in tasks such as image recognition for spotting cancerous tumours from MRI scans. Despite these improvements in performance of tasks such as image recognition, the underlying technology has not really changed since the 1980s and there have been no significant breakthroughs in understanding how to model intelligence. In fact, there's no understanding in the human cognitive sense taking place at all. Artificial intelligence is just that, artificial. It simulates only certain restricted aspects of human cognitive capabilities. On limited tasks this can leave people with the illusion that they're witnessing a machine as intelligent as they are! There is, however, no doubt that AI has appeared to advance rapidly since 2010. What lies behind this seeming advance?

What took so long?

When I was working in the field of computer speech and language understanding, there were three major limitations to advancing the capabilities of the technology and achieving the sort of commercialization that has been realized today, with products such as Amazon's

Alexa and Apple's Siri. These had limited computer power and memory and, perhaps most importantly, lack of training data.

The reason that AI, in the form described, has become so widespread is that computer power has been doubling every two years, along with computer memory capacity. During the five years that I was project director of the 20 million Euro, pan European research project on Spoken Dialogue Understanding (SUNDIAL),[6] we moved from using a large parallel array of microprocessor chips to a single processor.

When we tried to license this technology to ARM, then a local Cambridge company, which now supplies Apple and many other global companies with microprocessor chips, insufficient memory was available to run the software and store the statistical models needed for speech recognition. Since that time processors have become more than 3,000 times faster and memory capacity likewise has increased accordingly. It has also been discovered that the specialist graphics processing chips used in most computers are especially suited to the types of calculations needed to process neural network algorithms. Smartphone manufacturers such as Apple have developed their own processors, specifically for AI applications on the phone. This has further improved the commercialization of AI technology.

Perhaps the most significant development, though, has been the availability of vast amounts of data for training data-hungry neural networks. Performance or accuracy of neural networks increases with the amount of training data available for the systems to learn from. In the days when I was developing speech recognition systems we had to pay people to provide the speech samples needed to train our systems. There was also a limit to how much data could be economically and practically recorded and stored.

Fast-forward to today and the large corporations now invested in speech and language technology, such as Google, Apple and

6 J. Peckham, 'A New Generation of Spoken Dialogue Systems: Results and Lessons from the SUNDIAL Project', in Proceedings of the Third European Conference on Speech Communication and Technology, Berlin (1993), European Speech Communications Association, pp. 33–40.

Amazon, collect vast amounts of data every day, for free. This data is stored in massive memory banks the size of warehouses. Yet in 1994, just after the SUNDIAL project was completed, Amazon founder Jeff Bezos was only just staring his business in his garage in Bellevue, Washington, USA. In just over twenty years Amazon has grown to become a very powerful multinational company – for a brief period, along with Apple, worth more than 1 trillion US dollars in 2018, both surpassing Microsoft in valuation.

In his book *AI Super-Powers* Dr Kai-foo Lee, who did his doctorate in speech recognition at Carnegie Mellon University in the 1980s, claims that the field of AI is now in the age of implementation, rather than discovery.[7] This is because the technology and data available today have allowed many more applications to be created with the AI capabilities that we have. In addition, AI technology is just software that can easily be transferred from one computer to another and one country to another. Kai-foo Lee states that this is one of the reasons why countries such as China have been able to advance rapidly in the deployment of AI technology. It's also perhaps the reason why they plan to become the global leader in AI by 2030. In the first two decades of the twenty-first century investment in AI companies and research has increased exponentially, with funding running into tens of billions of dollars. For the first time, in 2017, China overtook the USA in the amount of funding provided for AI.

The world's our oyster

With the amount of hype surrounding AI over the last few years one might be forgiven for thinking that AI will take over the world, with machines becoming more intelligent than humans. Vladimir Putin, Russia's president, speaking to students in 2017 said:

> Artificial intelligence is the future, not only for Russia, but for all humankind, it comes with colossal opportunities, but also

7 K. Lee, *AI Superpowers: China, Silicon Valley and the New World Order* (New York: Houghton Mifflin Harcourt, 2018), p. 13.

> threats that are difficult to predict. Whoever becomes the leader in this sphere will become the ruler of the world.[8]

The Chinese government has said that it will invest heavily in AI, to ensure that its companies, government and military dominate the field by 2030. President Xi Jinping believes that being at the forefront in AI technology is critical in the competition for global military and economic power. China's State Council released a New Generation Artificial Intelligence Development Plan in 2015, where they state in the opening paragraph that

> AI has become a new focus of international competition. AI is a strategic technology that will lead in the future; the world's major developed countries are taking the development of AI as a major strategy to enhance national competitiveness and protect national security.[9]

China's claim that they have closed the gap between themselves and the USA in AI research and development and commercial AI products is probably a fair assessment, given that they're particularly good at implementing and commercializing what has already been developed. Such countries also have a chance to leapfrog other Western countries in the way in which AI is used, due to a lack of the ethical barriers that may exist in the use of fully autonomous lethal weapons. Most Western countries want to ban the development or at least the use of such technology.

The age of implementation

Speculation will no doubt continue for some time to come over whether AI will ever achieve human capabilities across a broad range

8 '"Whoever Leads in AI Will Rule the World": Putin to Russian Children on Knowledge Day', *RT* Question, 1 September 2017, retrieved on 3 September 2020 from <https://www.rt.com/news/401731-ai-rule-world-putin>.

9 Cited in G. C. Allen, 'Understanding China's AI Strategy: Clues to Chinese Strategic Thinking on Artificial Intelligence and National Security', *Center for a New American Security* (February 2019), p. 3.

of tasks, and if so in what time frame. I tend to agree with Kai-foo Lee in his assessment that we're in the age of implementation, rather than discovery. Indeed, some have suggested that we may soon be entering another 'AI winter' as disillusionment sets in, as it did in the 1980s, about our ability to realize the promise of AI.

What AI, or, to be more specific, neural networks, can currently do, given the increase in computing power and the availability of training data, is nonetheless impressive. A wide range of problems is potentially solvable using this technology, particularly when it requires only software and a computer rather than robotics.

Countries such as China see the technology as an opportunity to overtake other nations as they seek to modernize and deal with the challenges of a large population in urban centres, or as an opportunity to monitor their citizens without an army of people doing it. It's well known that in the former communist countries of Eastern and Central Europe people were encouraged to spy on one another and report 'failings' to the state. Now AI technology offers the potential to do this on a massive scale with far fewer people needed!

Although most of the talent in AI technology has been concentrated in the West in recent decades, the availability of 'open source' software from companies such as Google has made it possible for others to play catch-up. This has been not so much in the development of AI itself, but rather in the development of applications using the neural network concepts that have gradually been refined since the 1980s.

Academics have shared and published ideas for decades, so that information on the state of the art in AI has never been more accessible. This, coupled with the availability of free or commercial software, has made the development of AI applications more a software engineering task than a scientific one requiring a high level of expertise.

Competent software engineers should therefore be able to grasp the concepts quickly and provide the necessary training data to create an application. Developments in neural networks in the 1980s also contributed to the 'democratization' of the algorithms in making it much easier to train systems without the expert and knowledgeable input of developers.

Key to the success of current AI applications is the availability of large data sets for training. This has favoured applications where such data sets already exist, whether in healthcare, government departments, finance or people's social media and purchasing activity.

The limited pool of AI talent, as opposed to competent engineers, has however become more and more concentrated in the large companies that have an interest in the area and can pay the huge salaries needed to attract the top talent. While some in China feel that they may be limited by a lack of this top talent, Kai-foo Lee, who is based in China and now operates a venture capital fund for AI, does not believe that this will be the case. He may well be right, given the lack of theoretical ideas to advance AI beyond further tweaks and enhancements to neural network algorithms. Nevertheless, China, along with many other countries, has joined a race to try to develop and attract more talent through academic courses and grants to universities. The Vector Institute in Toronto, Canada, an independent research centre for whom Geoffrey Hinton is the chief scientific advisor, when it opened in 2017 needed ten times the number of AI experts Canada provides every year, illustrating the scale of the challenge.[10]

Despite their limitations, neural networks can be particularly good at certain types of pattern matching, such as image and speech recognition. A rapidly developing area is also the usefulness of neural networks in matching new information to previously collected information, whether people's spending patterns, the likelihood of an arrested person reoffending or even the likelihood of children being at risk in certain families.

There's potentially no data set that cannot be exploited to allow a computer to make judgements on whether someone should get a loan, the traffic light should turn red or there's a cancerous tumour in the brain. This gives rise to privacy concerns. Should my health

10 J. Somers, 'Is AI Riding a One Trick Pony?', *MIT Review*, 2017.

data be made available to an AI company? Should the technology giants be exploiting my social media and purchasing habits to push more products or potential friends in front of me?

The drive of the major companies, together with a small army of newly formed AI start-ups and seemingly endless funding, is pushing AI application rapidly ahead, whether we like it or not. Over the next few years there will hardly be any areas of our lives that won't be influenced by AI software, some for good, others more questionable.

Intelligent robotics will take longer to be rolled out, because much more development is needed. Whereas the AI software remains much the same as for computer data processing, the mechanical requirements of robots are often quite complex. Some robots are able to mimic the dexterity of human limbs so they can perform jobs such as stacking shelves just as well as a human. Yet they're expensive and will take longer to roll out than AI software applications that run on a general-purpose computer. The investment needed in deploying intelligent robots to replace humans will slow the take-up of this type of AI, but just as robots took over the manufacturing sector, in time so will intelligent robots find their way into this and other sectors threatening blue-collar jobs.

But what of the future for AI? Will we remain stuck in the age of implementation, or will AI reach new heights in capability, even surpassing human intelligence?

A singular event

Chief Technology Officer at Google, Ray Kurzweil, believes that by 2029 AI will pass a valid Turing test and achieve human levels of intelligence.

He also predicted in his book *The Singularity Is Near*, published in 2005, that a profound and disruptive transformation in human capability will occur in 2045, the 'Singularity', when computers will become much more intelligent than humans. This is often referred to as 'superintelligence' in AI circles.

Kurzweil's views are based on the belief that computer technology and our power to understand the human brain grows exponentially, so that computers become a million times more powerful in twenty years. This is a prediction similar to Moore's law for computer technology, which states that overall processing power for computers will double every two years.[11] This idea of so-called technology singularity goes back to the 1950s to the Hungarian-American mathematician and computer scientist John von Neumann. It's a hypothetical future point at which technological growth becomes uncontrollable and irreversible, 'beyond which human affairs, as we know them, could not continue'.[12]

A survey of expert opinion, conducted by Müller and Bostrom and published in 2016, found that only 50% believed that a high level of machine intelligence would be achieved between 2040 and 2050. Müller and Bostrom defined high-level machine intelligence as a machine 'that can carry out most human professions at least as well as a typical human'. However, when the dates for achieving this high level of machine intelligence are pushed further into the future, 90% believed that there was a likelihood of a high level of machine intelligence by 2075, and all believed that superintelligence would be created within thirty years or less from that point. Interestingly, only a third of the experts believed that this would result in a bad outcome for humanity.[13]

These sorts of predictions have resulted in a flurry of public debate and sensationalist books predicting the demise of civilization. Nick Bostrom, in the preface to his book *Superintelligence: Paths, Dangers, Strategies*, paints an alarming view of the future for civilization, should we ever develop super AI:

> If machine brains surpassed human brains in general intelligence, then this new superintelligence could become extremely powerful – possibly beyond our control. As the fate of the

11 See <www.mooreslaw.org> retrieved on 13 September 2020.

12 Reported by Stanislaw Ulam in his tribute to von Neumann after his death, S. Ulam, 'John von Neumann, 1903–1957', *Bulletin of the American Mathematical Society* 64 (3) part 2 (1958), p. 5. P. 5 retrieved on 11 September 2020 from <https://projecteuclid.org/download/pdf_1/euclid.bams/1183522369>.

13 V. Müller and N. Bostrom, 'Future Progress in Artificial Intelligence: A Survey of Expert Opinion', in *Fundamental Issues of Artificial Intelligence* (Berlin: Springer, 2016), p. 553.

> gorillas now depends more on humans than on the species itself, so would the fate of humankind depend on the actions of the machine superintelligence.[14]

Addressing the question of whether the default outcome is doom, Bostrom postulates that 'we can now begin to see the outlines of an argument for fearing that a plausible default outcome of the creation of machine superintelligence is existential catastrophe'.[15]

Various other public figures have also joined in the debate, announcing a bleak future for civilization, with what's usually regarded as the inevitable ultimate success in replicating human capabilities in AI. Elon Musk, founder of the well-known automated electric car manufacturer Tesla, said at the 2017 governors meeting in the USA, 'AI is a fundamental risk to the existence of human civilization.'[16]

The late Stephen Hawking, a well-known Cambridge theoretical physicist and cosmologist speaking at a Web summit in Portugal in the same year, also claimed that 'AI could be the worst event in the history of our civilization'.[17]

The concern that Musk and Hawking are raising is the impact that an AI machine equivalent to or better than human capability will have on humanity and society as we currently know it. What is this dystopian future, and how realistic is it?

Becoming gods

In his popular book *Homo Deus: A Brief History of Tomorrow*[18] Yuval Harari, a professor at the Hebrew University in Jerusalem, also

---

14 N. Bostrom, *Superintelligence: Paths, Dangers, Strategies* (Oxford: Oxford University Press, 2014), p. vii.

15 Ibid., p. 115.

16 S. Gibbs, 'Elon Musk: Regulate AI to Combat "Existential Threat" Before It's too Late', *The Guardian*, 17 July 2017, retrieved on 3 September 2020 from <https://www.theguardian.com/technology/2017/jul/17/elon-musk-regulation-ai-combat-existential-threat-tesla-spacex-ceo>.

17 B. Molina, 'Hawking: AI Could Be the "Worst Event in the History of Our Civilisation"', *USA Today*, 17 December 2019, retrieved on 3 September 2020 from <https://eu.usatoday.com/story/tech/talkingtech/2017/11/07/hawking-ai-could-worst-event-history-our-civilization/839298001>.

18 Y. N. Harari, *Homo Deus: A Brief History of Tomorrow* (London: Harvill Secker, 2016).

paints a rather bleak future for humankind. While not suggesting that any of them are inevitable, he gives three potential dystopian scenarios for the future. One is where the *Homo sapiens* species completely loses its economic value, another is where it becomes managed by AI and the final one is where humans become technologically enhanced. He sees humans essentially as algorithms shaped by their environment and making decisions deterministically or randomly:

> The idea that humans will always have a unique ability beyond the reach of non-conscious algorithms is just wishful thinking. The current scientific answer to this pipe dream can be summarised in three simple principles:
>
> 1. Organisms are algorithms. Every animal – including Homo sapiens – is an assemblage of organic algorithms shaped by natural selection over millions of years of evolution.
>
> 2. Algorithmic calculations are not affected by the materials from which the calculator is built. Whether an abacus is made of wood, iron, or plastic, two plus two beads equals four beads.
>
> 3. Hence there is no reason to think that organic substrates can do things that non-organic algorithms will never be able to replicate or surpass.[19]

The idea that humans can be reduced to algorithms is important, because his speculations about the future of humankind are based on this notion. He postulates that significant progress will be made in understanding these algorithms, so that they can ultimately be encoded into a machine. By this logic he suggests that humanity may be replaced by a superman or *Homo Deus* (a human god), either as a separate entity or as a human enhancement.

Although not dismissing consciousness as a development in the future, Harari notes that computers are intelligent but not yet conscious. The result of the dystopian future that he proposes is that we could become economically useless, a topic that we'll return to

19 Ibid., p. 319.

in a later chapter. He concludes the book with the question 'What will happen to society, politics and daily life when non-conscious but highly intelligent algorithms know us better than we know ourselves?'[20]

Reviewing the book in *The Guardian*, David Runciman acknowledges the idea that intelligence is uncoupled from consciousness and writes:

> We have already built machines – vast data-processing networks – that can know our feelings better than we know them ourselves: that's intelligence. Google – the search engine, not the company – doesn't have beliefs and desires of its own. It doesn't care what we search for and it won't feel hurt by our behaviour. But it can process our behaviour to know what we want before we know it ourselves. That fact has the potential to change what it means to be human.[21]

Not all scientists are as optimistic about the prospects of developing 'general AI', but those in academia and industry may find it difficult to paint a more sober picture publicly, in the light of the huge government grants and private funding available. The debate has highlighted some crucial issues that don't look as if they will be resolved any time soon.

Perhaps the biggest questions that remain unanswered are what intelligence is, and whether or not it's related to consciousness. Are we *really* just a collection of algorithms processing information from our sensors and making random or pre-determined decisions?

Shane Legg and Marcus Hutter, in a 2007 edition of the academic journal *Minds and Machines*, capture this issue succinctly when they report: 'A fundamental problem in artificial intelligence is that nobody really knows what intelligence is.'[22] Despite the relative

20 Ibid., p. 462.

21 D. Runciman, '*Homo Deus* by Yuval Noah Harari Review – How Data Will Destroy Human Freedom', *The Guardian*, 24 August 2016; retrieved 27 April 2020 from <https://www.theguardian.com/books/2016/aug/24/homo-deus-by-yuval-noah-harari-review>.

22 S. Legg and M. Hutter, 'Universal Intelligence: A Definition of Machine Intelligence', *Minds and Machines* 17 (4) (2007), p. 391.

optimism of scientists such as Ray Kurzweil, the late Paul Allen, co-founder of Microsoft, took a more realistic view of the real prospects for general AI when he stated:

> Creating this kind of advanced software requires a prior scientific understanding of the foundations of human cognition, and we are just scraping the surface of this. This prior need to understand the basic science of cognition is where the 'singularity is near' arguments fail to persuade us.[23]

While AI may simulate more and more human functions, where machines can converse with us and even solve problems, is it really intelligent, able to think and reason freely as we do?

I think that the answer is no, because no one yet understands how to define intelligence in a way that would allow it to be codified. At present we simply don't know how a computer could be developed with the broad reasoning capabilities that humans readily display.

Even more intriguing is the question of whether AI will ever appear to be conscious. That requires us to understand what consciousness is before we could codify it. At this point it's worth pausing to reflect on what consciousness is. Is it physical or spiritual (metaphysical)? Answering that question will help us to understand whether it will ever be possible to codify it.

More than a memory

We all know that we have it, but how do we define it? British philosopher John Locke published an essay in 1689, 'Concerning Human Understanding', in which he defined consciousness as 'the perception of what passes in a man's own mind'. French philosopher René Descartes believed that the mind and the body were separate, a so-called mind–body dualism now referred to as 'Cartesian dualism'. He proposed that the reality of our existence is rooted in the notion

23 P. Allen and M. Greaves, 'Paul Allen: The Singularity Isn't Near', 12 October 2011, retrieved on 3 September 2020 from <https://www.technologyreview.com/2011/10/12/190773/paul-allen-the-singularity-isnt-near>.

'I think, therefore I am'. Descartes believed that consciousness exists in the non-material realm of our thought.

Even more difficult than defining consciousness precisely is developing a robust theory of where it comes from. Our world view has a strong influence on our answers to this question and whether it may be possible to emulate consciousness. Those who see consciousness as emerging from the development of the brain's neuronal patterns, as a baby grows into a child, will no doubt assume that it's only a matter of time before we develop a theory and mathematical model of this process, one that could then be encoded in a computer. Others who see the divine hand in giving us a soul in God's creation of man may well conclude differently.

In the twentieth century philosophers saw the problems to be solved in developing a theory of consciousness as two related problems. The first, 'how the brain generates the movie in the brain', and the second, how the brain generates 'the appearance of an owner and observer for the movie within the movie'.[24] Putting it another way, the 'hard problem', as Australian philosopher David Chalmers calls it, is how the material brain produces subjective experiences.[25]

There seems to be a sharp division between philosophers and cognitive neuroscientists who want to define consciousness without the Subject (the self), and those who say that if you leave out the Subject, then the theory is disqualified. As Fodor puts it, 'If, in short, there is a community of computers living in my head, there had also better be somebody who is in charge; and, by God, it had better be me.'[26]

Philosopher Daniel Dennett brings this dilemma into sharp focus when he says, 'This is not just my problem; it confronts anybody attempting to construct and defend a properly naturalistic, materialistic theory of consciousness.'[27]

24 D. Dennett, 'Are We Explaining Consciousness Yet?', *Cognition* 79 (2001), p. 228.

25 D. J. Chalmers, 'Facing up to the Problem of Consciousness', *Journal of Consciousness Studies* 2 (3) 1995, p. 200.

26 J. Fodor, 'Review of Steven Pinker's *How the Mind Works*, and Henry Plotkin's *Evolution in Mind*', *London Review of Books* (22 January 1998). Reprinted in Fodor, *In Critical Condition* (Cambridge, Mass.: MIT Press/Bradford Books, 1998), p. 207, cited in D. Dennett, 'Are We Explaining Consciousness Yet?', *Cognition* 79 (2001), p. 229.

27 Ibid., p. 229.

Therein lies the fundamental problem when trying to define or develop a theory of consciousness. If we take a materialistic world view and merely see humans as computers, then we'll struggle to accept what's obvious for a Christian: that we're more than just cells. Philosopher David Chalmers puts it this way:

> But on the most common conception of consciousness, it is not easy to see how it could be part of the physical world. So it seems that to find a place for consciousness within the natural order, we must either revise our conception of consciousness, or revise our conception of nature.[28]

The very idea of human consciousness and the mind, along with our difficulty in defining and understanding them, leads atheist philosopher Thomas Nagel to conclude that a materialist interpretation of evolutionary biology is unable to account for the mind and consciousness.[29] As one might expect, his book came in for a lot of criticism from fellow atheists, unwilling to accept the challenge that evolutionary theory 'flies in the face of common sense'.[30]

While philosophers continue to debate what consciousness is, two mainstream theories of how it's created are emerging from neuroscientists' study of the brain. One is that of 'Integrated Information Theory': over time our conscious experience represents the integration of information from our sensors and cognitive processes, such as emotion, and this cannot be changed by choice. We cannot, for example, choose to see in black and white. This theory means that consciousness cannot be broken down into constituent parts, and that no computer simulation could ever become conscious.

The other theory of consciousness proposed by neuroscientists is the 'Global Workspace Theory', where, rather like computer memory, our brain is able to store experiences and call them up after they have passed. This theory uses an old concept in symbolic AI, or expert

28 D. Chalmers, 'Consciousness and Its Place in Nature', in S. P. Stich and T. A. Warfield (eds), *Blackwell Guide to the Philosophy of Mind* (Oxford: Blackwell, 2003), p. 102.

29 T. Nagel, *Mind and Cosmos: Why the Materialist Neo-Darwinian Conception of Nature Is Almost Certainly False* (Oxford: Oxford University Press, 2012).

30 Ibid., pp. 5–6.

systems, called 'the blackboard' – a memory space that different programs can access. According to this theory, the broadcasting around the brain of the information stored in the 'blackboard', whether a childhood experience, one's reaction to flying for the first time or a first date, is what consciousness is. On this view, computers could, in theory, become conscious by having a very large 'blackboard' in which experiences and memories are stored and broadcast to other programs.

So, where does all this speculation about intelligence and consciousness leave us? AI is based on very simplistic pattern-matching and pattern-detecting algorithms that do not really model even the limited understanding that we have about how the brain works. The reality is that we have no widely accepted definition of intelligence or consciousness, nor whether the two are disconnected.

Although a computer algorithm may appear intelligent, it's only an appearance or perception, based on its ability to perform some task at least as well as, or better than, a human. There's no reasoning involved nor understanding of the tasks being carried out, no consciousness of itself. One might ask: does the fact that a digging machine can perform far better than a man with a spade make it intelligent?

Clearly, there's some difference of view among scientists as to whether we'll ever be able to create a machine with the same level of intelligence as a human, or when that might occur. What's clear is that predictions are being made on the basis of the rate of advances in technology and a naturalistic understanding of how humans function rather than on any concrete notion of how to create such a machine.

Our beliefs about humanity, whether we're just a collection of biological algorithms or something more, has a significant bearing on what sort of AI we think it may be possible to create in the future.

Whatever the future holds for AI technology, what's more pressing is the impact that today's technology is already having on what it means to be human. Before we turn to look at that question in more detail, we need first to explore whether technology itself is neutral, in the sense of its moral and ethical impact on us. Second, we need to explore what the Bible teaches us about being human, in order to view correctly and understand how AI and digital technology might influence us, and whether this is for good or bad. Let's begin by exploring whether technology is value neutral, and whether what really matters is how we use it.

3
A mistaken neutrality

Generally, technologists, including myself, have tended to assert that technology is neutral. What we do with it determines whether it's good or bad. This has been convenient for both technologists and companies that sell technology, for such an assertion brooks no argument. It absolves us of any moral responsibility for what we invent.

I am now much less convinced by this argument and believe that the answer to the question 'Is technology neutral?' is rather more nuanced. While it's true that we can do both good and bad things with technology, the important question isn't whether technology is moral but rather whether its very existence and design influence human behaviour.

As I argue in later chapters, technology is an artefact that we create and as such has no moral agency. Nor should we accord it any. On this basis it cannot be moral. Yet it's clear from history that it has had a profound impact on society and individuals. The information age of the late twentieth century has ushered in changes at an unprecedented pace in human history. Society has had no time to pause and consider the impact of the internet, social media, cryptocurrency, and even less AI, on humanity.

To print or not to print?

The invention of the printing press provides an early example of the different ways in which people thought of disruptive technology. Johannes Gutenberg, who invented the printing press in Europe in the 1430s, met strong opposition from some who saw their work being replaced. Johannes Trithemius, an influential German

Benedictine abbot, cryptographer and occultist, argued for the moral supremacy of handwriting over mechanical printing in a tract written in 1492:

> He who gives up copying because of the invention of printing is no genuine friend of Holy Scripture. He sees only what is and contributes nothing to the edification of future generations. But we beloved brothers shall keep in mind the reward of this sacred occupation and not slacken our efforts, even if we were to own many thousands of books. Printed books will never be the equivalent of handwritten codices, especially since printed books are often deficient in spelling and appearance. The simple reason is that copying by hand involves more diligence and industry.[1]

Trithemius died in 1516, a year before Martin Luther nailed his Ninety-five Theses to the church door at Wittenberg, leading to the Reformation and eventually the printing of the Bible in the common language of the people. Perhaps Trithemius was concerned about monks losing their jobs, but in any event he did not see the printing press as morally neutral!

Changing culture

Political theorist Langdon Winner, Thomas Phelan Chair of Humanities and Social Sciences at Rensselaer Polytechnic Institute in Troy, New York, made this observation in 1986, in his study of technology out of control:

> If the experience of modern society shows us anything, however, it is that technologies are not merely aids to human activity, but also powerful forces acting to reshape that activity and its meaning. The introduction of a robot to an industrial

1 J. Trithemius, *In Praise of Scribes (De laude scriptorum)*, trans. R. Behrendt (Lawrence, Kans.: Coronado Press, 1974), p. 475, retrieved on 6 September 2019 from <http://williamwolff.org/wp-content/uploads/2009/06/TrithemiusScribes.pdf>.

> workplace not only increases productivity but often radically changes the process of production, redefining what work means in that setting. When a sophisticated new technique or instrument is adopted in medical practice, it transforms not only what doctors do but also the ways people think about health, sickness and medical care. Widespread alterations of this kind in techniques of communication, transportation, manufacturing, agriculture, and the like are largely what distinguishes our times from early periods of human history.[2]

If technology does influence us individually and we see it also influencing our society, then isn't the answer just to choose not to use those technologies that we consider to have harmful effects? This brings us back to the neutrality argument that says it's what we do with it that counts. Reflecting on the role that television plays in society and how much time Americans spend watching it, Winner suggests it's no longer as simple as just choosing to turn it off:

> Those who wish to reassert freedom of choice in the matter sometimes observe, you can always turn off your TV. In a trivial sense that is true . . . But given how central television has become to the content of everyday life, how it has become the accustomed topic of conversation at workplaces, schools, and other social gatherings, it is apparent that television is a phenomenon that, in the larger sense, cannot be 'turned off' at all. Deeply insinuated into people's perceptions, thoughts, and behaviour, it has become an indelible part of modern culture.[3]

The reality is that the availability of technology itself has a profound influence on individuals and society. Put a gun in your hand and the balance of power changes. It now becomes so much easier to kill someone, as the spate of shootings in the USA and elsewhere powerfully illustrates. Clearly, the perpetrators were disturbed,

2 L. Winner, *The Whale and the Reactor: A Search for Limits in an Age of High Technology* (Chicago: University of Chicago Press, 1986), p. 7.

3 Ibid., p. 12.

criminals or terrorists and their intention was to do bad things with the weapons. The fact is, however, that access to powerful weapons gave them more options for evil.

Weapons are created for a purpose: to kill people. And while we might see that as positive in the context of winning a just war, the manufacturers are less concerned with who uses weapons and how they're used than with sales. Guns fall into the hands of terrorists, criminals and juveniles, even innocents who accidentally set off a gun and kill or maim a family member or friend. Even if we're to concede that weapons are needed as a deterrent and are an important component of winning a just war and ensuring peace, ethical questions still surround their use, such as: whose peace and what's a just war?

This piece of technology isn't neutral in its influence: it was designed to take life, and that means that it comes laden with the values and world view of its creators and manufacturers. I could use a gun as an effective doorstop or hang it in a glass case to look at, but that's not what it was made for.

The printing press is an early example of the way in which whole societies and cultures both in Europe and Asia were shaped through the influence of the printed word. The ability to get the message out to many people, previously not feasible with handwriting, enabled many in Europe to hear of Luther's theses and concerns about the Catholic Church. Yet some of the violence that resulted was not the outcome Luther desired.

The printing press eventually allowed ordinary people to read the Bible in their own language instead of its being the preserve of the educated priest, who could read Latin. That was surely a good outcome!

Take another example of how technology changes culture. Monks first rang bells and then used early developments of the mechanical clock at the beginning of the fourteenth century to enable them to keep the canonical course of their liturgy. The development of time-keeping, both the habit and the devices that could mark out the passage of time, eventually revolutionized European economies, leading to the Industrial Revolution. As David Landes puts it in his influential book *Revolution in Time*, 'Punctuality comes from within, not from without. It is the mechanical clock that made possible, for better or worse, a civilization attentive to the passage of time, hence to productivity and performance.'[4]

Technology expands the possibilities available to us and in so doing immediately offers us choices – choices that humans are sometimes bad at making. We could choose to do the right thing but sin crouches at the door.

A hidden addiction

While not going so far as to talk about sin, philosopher David Morrow argues that for two reasons technology isn't value neutral. Either it induces short-sighted behaviour, rather than valuing future benefits, or it creates or exacerbates collective behaviour problems.[5] For most, instant gratification trumps doing something that will bear fruit later. So, with the best will in the world, we might prefer to spend an hour online rather than spend the time practising the instrument we've been wanting to learn for years, or doing the boring chores that await!

Morrow cites overfishing as an example of where technology creates a 'collective behaviour problem'. Although there are rules in place, the tendency is for selfish accumulation at the expense of others seeking to fish in the same waters. Overfishing occurs because of the efficiency with which factory ships operate. It would be an unlikely problem if fishermen were just using a fishing rod.

While technology is neutral, in the sense that an artefact possesses no inherent values or moral agency, there cannot be a neutral reaction to its use, especially in the case of what we might call 'digital technology'. This is because it has been designed by people with values and a world view that shape its purpose and functionality.

4 D. S. Landes, *Revolution in Time: Clocks and the Making of the Modern World* (Cambridge, Mass.: Belknap/Harvard University Press, 1983), p. 7.

5 D. R. Morrow, 'When Technologies Make Good People Do Bad Things: Another Argument Against the Value-Neutrality of Technologies', *Science and Engineering Ethics* 20 (2) (2013), pp. 329–343.

In the case of AI, the algorithms require data to learn how to pattern-match and this can exacerbate the influence of the creator because, as we'll see later, this data is often biased, sometimes by race or gender.

Google Duplex is a research and design project to allow people to ask a digital assistant to make appointments or book restaurants by itself. When you listen to sales talks and techies talking excitedly about this and other products, such as the iPhone, the talk is all about making life better, more convenient. But at what cost and who really benefits? My point is that while the techies may genuinely be excited about their inventions, the corporations who pay them have profits, not human benevolence, in mind.

Because that's what drives income from their advertisers, the big companies behind AI have one goal in mind: increasing traffic and usage of their platforms. The more people become addicted to their convenient digital assistants, the greater the revenue these companies make, with most people unaware of how they're being exploited.

While the technology may offer convenience, it has been designed thus and to create addiction for the purpose not of making one's life easier but of driving profits. One might argue, 'What's wrong with that? Don't all products in a free market work in that way?' We buy something because it offers us a benefit, and naturally the company that sold it to us profits. The distinction here is that some products, some technologies, appear to do that, but are by their design exploiting our vulnerabilities, influencing us as individuals and as a society in ways that are diminishing what it means to be human. A bread toaster is convenient and useful in the kitchen, but it hardly affects what it means to be a human being, except when we burn our fingers trying to extract the toast!

My thesis, then, is that technology isn't neutral in its effect on people for two reasons. The first is that technology is designed and sold by people for a purpose, and that purpose is laden with values and a world view. Rarely are these values purely benign, because profits are needed to fund research. Profits come from products that people want to buy, or from third parties such as advertisers, when products or services are offered for free, as Facebook and Google do.

The second reason that technology isn't neutral in its effect is that users are fallible people and products are designed to offer us more possibilities. They suck us in by exploiting human weakness, the vices such as greed, vanity, lust, insecurity and anger. A consequence of the impact of technology on individuals is that culture is eventually shaped by it as more and more are drawn in. The world has never before experienced such a rapid shaping of cultures due to the accelerating development of digital technologies such as the internet and AI.

New is better than old

Behind the seduction of digital technology and AI is the Enlightenment idea that progress is good and progress is driven by science and technology. The Age of Enlightenment began in eighteenth-century Europe and gradually spread around the world, fuelling the Industrial Revolution and the free-market economies of the West. Human reason was seen as the source of knowledge, and progress would be achieved through scientific discovery and empiricism. French philosophers championed the idea of individual liberty and the separation of the state from religion.

Today science and technology are widely seen as the drivers of progress that will allow humanity to flourish. These ideas are embedded in much of our thinking and behaviour regarding new technology. New is better than old – we've all watched the queues for the latest iPhone, every time hailed as 'the best iPhone we've produced'.

It's not surprising therefore that there's an assumption that AI technology is good, that it will make our lives easier and more comfortable, and that it will enable humanity to flourish. Businesses strive for greater efficiencies, and we become people driven by what's convenient, without ever asking what we're losing and what this technology is doing to us.

Taken to its extreme, the transhumanist philosophy that many leaders of hi-tech companies subscribe to is nothing less than the transformation of the human condition through technology, including AI. Followers of this philosophy see the potential for humanity to be transformed into different beings, posthumans, with greater abilities than mere humans, even potentially defying death through genetic engineering, drug therapy or uploading one's brain.[6]

Losing consciousness

An assumption that technology represents progress and that progress must be good has dulled our consciousness of whether it's right. We engage with social media, the internet, online shopping and the latest gadgets without ever pausing to think about what it may be doing to the image of God in us, or how it may be changing our behaviour and relationships.

The fast pace of change is making us breathless and restless for the next new thing, so that we expect to move from job to job and even relationship to relationship, looking for something new, something better, something that will leave us more fulfilled. Churches feel the need to innovate so as not to seem old and stale, to attract the younger trendy set who are constantly on the move. Mission embraces social media and other digital technologies without stopping to think about the values being supported or the data being farmed. Church leaders tweet their thoughts to millions and publishers want their articles liked and the pithy quote retweeted.

We need to step back, pause and regain consciousness of what's happening around us. Not necessarily to discard new technology, but rather to engage it with informed minds – minds that have a clear view of whether it helps or hinders our walk with God, our relationships with others and our desire to become more like Christ.

How does technology, AI as we now know it and as it will develop in the next few decades, influence our image bearing as people made in God's image? In order to help us answer this question we need to remind ourselves of all that it means to be made in his image.

6 See chapter 10 below.

4
Totally amazing!

I've argued that technology isn't neutral, in that it changes us as we engage with it, whether we like it or not. This arises not only from the intentions of the inventor and the business supplying the technology, but also from the new possibilities that it opens up. All of this is taking place in the context of an Enlightenment world view that champions progress as the determiner of happiness and human flourishing.

Science and technology are seen as the drivers of progress. If it's more efficient or convenient, it must be better: new is better than old. A new iPhone is better than the one in my pocket, even though it's only a year old. When we make decisions about using technology, rarely do we stop to ask whether it's right and what 'right' would mean in relation to choosing whether or not to engage with technology.

These factors, together with the way in which digital technology is so often designed to appeal to our vulnerabilities, are transforming our behaviours and influencing what it means to be human. We've seen that we're gradually losing our consciousness of what's happening to us and are at risk of being swept along by the culture around us. The alluring advertising messages from Big Tech lull us into a sense of comfort, security and entitlement.

In order to determine how digital technologies, and AI applications in particular, are shaping us we need to step back and remind ourselves of what it means to be a human created in God's image. We need to remind ourselves of what God has called us to be, and ask how that's helped or hindered by the technology around us, and particularly AI.

Made in God's image

Right from the opening chapter of the Bible we learn that we're created in God's image when God said:

> Let us make man in our image, after our likeness. And let them have dominion over the fish of the sea and over the birds of the heavens and over the livestock and over all the earth and over every creeping thing that creeps on the earth.
> (Gen. 1:26)

In God's creating activity, man and woman are singled out from the animals and the rest of physical creation as special, because nowhere else in Scripture is anything else that God creates defined as in his 'image' or 'likeness'. The Hebrew terms for 'image' (*ṣelem*, meaning 'statue', 'image' or 'copy') and 'likeness' (*dĕmût*, meaning 'likeness', 'pattern') are essentially synonymous: they amount to the same thing. Although some have sought to create a distinction between them, it's most likely that the two terms were used for literary effect, emphasizing that we were made as a reflection or mirror of God. We're made after the pattern of God or resembling him.

But what does it really mean to be made in his image or likeness? To get to grips with this, we need to understand something about the essence of God.

What is the essence of God?

God does not manifest himself in physical form: he's metaphysical and this therefore means that we in some way mirror his essence or nature, both through our body and what we call the soul. This raises the questions: what is the essence of God, what is he like and how are we like him?

What we know about God comes from his self-disclosure, by inspiring authors to write the ancient texts, assembled now into what we call the Bible. From these texts we can build a picture of what God is like and can thus describe him as having certain attributes, such as holiness, love, mercy, justice, righteousness and intellect.

He's a God who thinks and reasons. Some theologians like to group these attributes into categories such as goodness – embracing attributes such as love, mercy, righteousness, justice and holiness. The category of knowledge covers the attributes of speech, reason, truth and wisdom. God's power is yet another category that covers his eternal being, existence, omnipresence and immensity.[1] All of these attributes are of course part and parcel of who God is, and any divisions are merely human attempts to try to define what he's like. What we can say overall is that these attributes encompass God's moral excellence.

Observation of humans shows that they too possess similar attributes to God. Humankind can love, show mercy, reason and think. But is this what it means to be made 'in God's image'? The topic has been a subject of debate and study since the early church fathers and continues unabated to this day.

The church fathers were the first to study more thoroughly what *Imago Dei* (image of God) means, and Tertullian saw free will as the essential mark or stamp of the divine image. Augustine suggested that God and humans share some ontological[2] component, trait or quality that essentially defines us: memory, intelligence and will.

Varying views were held among the Reformers and Reformed theologians, but the dominant view has been that there's both a narrow and a broad definition of what it means to be made in God's image. The narrow definition describes a spiritual dimension, or the virtues of holiness, knowledge of the truth and righteousness that humans possessed before the fall. In the narrow definition this divine image was lost in the fall of humankind and could be reclaimed only through redemption. However, a broader view of *Imago Dei* accepts that humans possess other attributes of God, such as intelligence, natural affections and freedom to choose, and that these are retained by all of humanity.[3] The idea that we're moral beings because we're made in the likeness of a moral God is

1 J. Frame, *The Doctrine of God* (Phillipsburg, N.J.: P&R Publishing, 2002), p. 399.
2 The essence or nature of being.
3 L. Berkhof, *Systematic Theology* (Edinburgh: Banner of Truth Trust, 1976), p. 204.

important in our consideration of how AI might influence our ability to image or mirror the God who made us.

Adam and Eve had moral freedom. They chose, against God's command, to eat the fruit of the tree of the knowledge of good and evil when they were tempted in the garden of Eden. Moral freedom, or free will – the freedom to choose a course of action – is a fundamental aspect of being made in God's image and has significant implications for how we view some aspects of AI deployment. It's also a concept challenged by some, so we'll return to this topic a little later in the chapter. For now we've established that men and women are created with freedom to choose, and this is a fundamental part of being human, made in the likeness of God. Furthermore, God holds us accountable to him and liable for the actions that we take, judged against his standards of moral excellence, also explicitly communicated in his Word.

There are a number of other consequences of God's being moral in character. One in particular is his unconditional love, a love that has meaning only *because* he has freedom to choose to love. This love is shown supremely in God's love for fallen humans in sending his Son, Jesus Christ, to suffer and die for our sins. We too share the ability to love, because we're made in his image.

Although there was love and communion between God and Adam, God desired that man should have a human companion, so he brought forth woman from Adam's rib. They were able to enjoy love for each other and intimate sexual union as one flesh. True love stems from God's moral nature and requires freedom to choose to love, or it's not love at all.

Turning to the category of knowledge, which sums up other aspects of God's attributes, we see that he's a God of reason. That part of the nature of God is clearly mirrored in human beings. Knowledge is a part of who he is, a reasoning, logical and intelligent God who is truth. That he's a reasoning God is seen in Isaiah's vision concerning Judah and Jerusalem, where God communicates his view of the waywardness of his people. God nonetheless encourages them to repentance and forgiveness with the words 'Come now, let us reason together, says the LORD' (Isa. 1:18).

Our ability to reason is a precious part of what it means to be human. It's special to us and we don't see it mirrored in animals. This ability to reason is communicated in language, both spoken and written, at a level unique to humans. We see reason worked out in Adam's relationship and communion with God, in his understanding of what God was telling him and acting upon it – such as in naming the animals that God brought before him. Speech is the primary way in which God communicates truth, his word, to men and women.

Another aspect of defining the nature of God is that the act of creation itself shows us that he's a God who works and creates. Work was also part of God's design for humankind and clearly a part of the natural order when he created Adam and Eve and they tilled and kept the garden. We'll explore this theme more thoroughly in chapter 9.

Right at the very beginning of creation, then, we're able to see clearly the outworking of being made in God's image: our mirroring or patterning of his nature. Man and woman are gloriously and amazingly imaging the very essence of God's nature. Having the freedom to choose, love, reason, communicate, work and create, they're imaging his being.

Clearly the fall of humankind, described in Genesis 3, changes what we're like because of the introduction of the corrupting power of sin. No longer do we love perfectly or think completely rationally, no longer do we seek justice and righteousness as God does, because of our selfish desires.

The apostle Paul argues in his letter to the Roman Christians that

> his invisible attributes, namely, his eternal power and divine nature, have been clearly perceived, ever since the creation of the world, in the things that have been made. So they are without excuse. For although they knew God, they did not honour him as God or give thanks to him, but they became futile in their thinking, and their foolish hearts were darkened. Claiming to be wise, they became fools, and exchanged the

> glory of the immortal God for images resembling mortal man and birds and animals and creeping things.
> (Rom. 1:20–23)

A consequence of this rejection of God is that we do not think as we were created to think: we become futile in our thinking. The ultimate rejection of God by humans causes him to give them up to a 'debased mind to do what ought not to be done' (Rom. 1:28).

Nonetheless, we remain creatures made in his image, made of his essence, and some of the nature of God is still seen, even in fallen humankind. This image begins to be restored when we're redeemed by Christ. Paul says to the Colossian Christians that they're to be renewed after the image of their creator (Col. 3:10). From this perspective we can see that a Christian should, to a greater extent than others, display characteristics of God's nature, his moral freedom shown in love and compassion for others, kindness, a desire for justice and doing the right thing. We should not be those whom Paul speaks of, who are foolish in their thinking, but those who are able to reason and use our intellect, patterned after God. Perhaps the best way of thinking about fallen humanity and the *Imago Dei* is the way Francis Schaeffer once expressed it, as 'a glorious ruin'.

As those who are redeemed by the work of Christ on the cross, it now not only becomes possible to be virtuous, to show those attributes of God lost by us and tarnished in the fall, but it's also commanded. We're to become partakers of the divine nature:

> His divine power has granted to us all things that pertain to life and godliness, through the knowledge of him who called us to his own glory and excellence, by which he has granted to us his precious and very great promises, so that through them you may become partakers of the divine nature, having escaped from the corruption that is in the world because of sinful desire. For this very reason, make every effort to supplement your faith with virtue, and virtue with knowledge, and knowledge with self-control, and self-control with

> steadfastness, and steadfastness with godliness, and godliness with brotherly affection, and brotherly affection with love.
> (2 Peter 1:3–7)

As we'll see in later chapters, this doctrine is key to how we view AI and its impact on us: whether it helps or hinders our growth in virtue, self-control and godliness.

What we've seen so far is that *Imago Dei* means being made as a mirror of the nature of God. This has to do with reflecting some of God's attributes, such as being moral, having freedom to choose and to reason.

In the twentieth century theologians began to challenge the ontological view, or what we might call 'the attributes of God', as what's meant by being created in his image. They argued that *Imago Dei* is more about the function of humans, what we're made to *do*, rather than what we *are* or what attributes we display. This view sees humankind as agents or representatives of God rather than sharing his attributes. For convenience I've called this the functional view. This view, however, is really more about what we do as people made in God's likeness, and in my view it would be a mistake to see it as an alternative meaning of *Imago Dei*. It does not replace the understanding that we've so far explored of what being made in his image or likeness means. Indeed, what we've discussed so far is fundamental to a full understanding of what it means to be human.

Rather than being an alternative view of *Imago Dei*, I would suggest that the functional view simply enriches our understanding of what it means to be human. For this reason, we'll explore this view in a little more detail.

What we're made for

The functional role rests on an alternative translation of Genesis 1:26, 'let us make humanity *as* our image',[4] but it's also supported by the second part of Genesis 1:26, where God says, 'And let them

4 T. D. Alexander and D. W. Baker, *Dictionary of the Old Testament, Pentateuch* (Downers Grove: InterVarsity Press; Leicester: Inter-Varsity Press, 2003), pp. 443–444.

have dominion'. This verse is essentially saying that humans are to have dominion over all that he has created, whether living or non-living. This view of *Imago Dei* is one of humankind being delegated by God to oversee his creation as his vicegerent.[5]

The idea of being a vicegerent comes from the ancient rule of kings over their kingdom and people, with the vicegerent being appointed to co-govern or rule. In ancient times a king might have had statues (icons) erected to remind his subjects who was king and lord over them. In ancient Egyptian and Mesopotamian texts kings were seen as sons of gods and therefore being in the god's image. This is an interesting motif when we consider the biblical texts that also speak of Adam's being a 'son of God' (Luke 3:38). Being in God's image carries with it the idea of sonship and sons representing our Father on earth in his cosmic temple.

This idea of image bearing or of being 'icons' of God in his creation is a powerful one, especially in the context of thinking about ways our image bearing might be tarnished by the use of AI technology.

The image that we're to mirror or display links back to what we learnt about the nature of God and the attributes that we share. We must therefore be careful not to allow our humanity to be 'downgraded'. Ex-Google ethicist Tristan Harris has popularized this term to describe the way in which smartphones affect humanity. Harris cites a number of ways in which humanity is being dumbed down by technology designed to grab more and more of our attention. This results in an interconnected set of issues such as shortening attention spans, social isolation, polarization of views along with manipulation and addiction brought about by the use of techniques such as notifications.

The functional view of being made in God's image goes beyond the idea of being an icon, something that should look like the one it represents. To exercise dominion over God's creation isn't a passive thing. It carries with it the responsibility to work and be creative: we see that even before the fall God put humans in a garden to till and

5 For an extended treatment of this view see J. R. Middleton, *The Liberating Image: The* Imago Dei *in Genesis 1* (Grand Rapids: Brazos Press, 2005).

keep it: 'The LORD God took the man and put him in the garden of Eden to work it and keep it' (Gen. 2:15).

Keeping the garden implies caring for it and by extension caring for the whole kingdom, its people and territory, with the same care that the ruler would exercise.

The exploitation of our natural resources, and the sometimes devastating consequences on habitats and the environment, has spurred many in the last few decades to adopt the functional view of *Imago Dei*. This translates into Christians both encouraging others and themselves leading the way in being better stewards of our natural resources by caring for the environment and avoiding species extinction. This view of *Imago Dei* is often referred to as the 'creation mandate', where God covenants with Adam and his offspring to hold them responsible for the management of his creation. The creation mandate is also seen by some as the spur for Christians to engage with culture and be 'culture makers' as part of the process of bringing in the kingdom or restoring creation.

The functional view of *Imago Dei* emphasizes the purpose for which we're made: humanity's function. Rather than standing opposed to the view that we share some of the attributes of God, it underscores our need to ensure that we reflect that image. The icon bears witness to the one whom it represents. Going further, the vicegerent has a responsibility to function in a way consistent with the nature of our creator, whose image we bear.

There's still yet another way in which *Imago Dei* may be interpreted, and once more we'll see that, rather than being an alternative view, it complements and enriches the understanding of *Imago Dei* I've already described.

When we read the familiar creation texts in Genesis, and especially that which speaks of the creation of humans, it's all too easy to miss that the three persons of the Trinity were involved. God said 'let *us* make man in *our* image' (Gen. 1:26; italics mine). The nature of the image that we've been exploring thus far is the image of all three persons of the Trinity.

In the Trinity we see a perfect relationship and God's creating man ultimately for relationship with himself: Father, Son and Holy Spirit.

This, in addition to the ontological and functional views described previously, leads to a third view of what's meant by being created in God's image. It's about humankind being created for relationship with God, what Martin Buber describes in his 1923 book *Ich und Du* (*I and Thou*) as the 'I–Thou' relationship.[6] This extends to relationships between man and woman and our 'neighbour'. For convenience I've described this as the relationship view.

Made for relationship

The relational view of *Imago Dei* centres around the idea that God created us for relationship, just as the Trinity is in relationship. So humans are created to be in relationship with the Trinity, but also with other human beings, seen especially in the companion created to be Adam's wife. In this relationship we see an intimacy expressed through their becoming 'one flesh'. The relational purpose of God's creating humankind is born out in Jesus' answer to the scribe's question as to what the most important commands are:

> The most important is, 'Hear, O Israel: The Lord our God, the Lord is one. And you shall love the Lord your God with all your heart and with all your soul and with all your mind and with all your strength.' The second is this: 'You shall love your neighbour as yourself.' There is no other commandment greater than these.
> (Mark 12:29–31)

From this we can see clearly that humans were created for relationship, to love and obey God; and if we're a Christian, this becomes the main goal in our lives, along with loving our neighbour as ourselves.

Which of these views of *Imago Dei* is correct and do we have to choose? As I've already mentioned, I believe that all three are correct and valuable interpretations of Scripture, when taken in context with Scripture as a whole. They're in fact different facets of the *Imago Dei*,

6 M. Buber, *I and Thou*, trans. Ronald Gregor-Smith (New York: Scribner, 1984).

what it means to be created in God's image. Figure 1 illustrates the three views that I've described and their different emphases. Each conveys a different aspect of what is unique about us and what it means to be human.

Then God said, 'Let us make man in our image, after our likeness. And let them have dominion over the fish of the sea and over the birds of the heavens and over the livestock and over all the earth and over every creeping thing that creeps on the earth.' (Gen. 1:26)

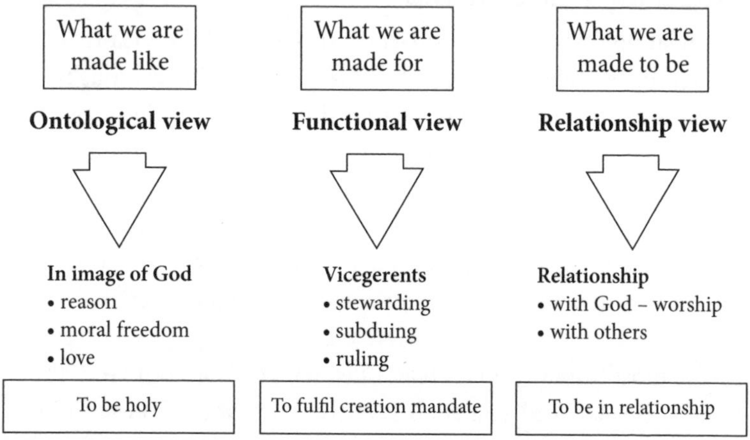

Figure 1 **What makes us special – three views of the *Imago Dei***

Each of the three views of *Imago Dei* has a special contribution to the development of Christian ethics in regard to AI and its deployment, as we'll see in later chapters. This third view, the relationship view, helps us to question whether my use of this technology affects the way in which I relate to people – does it diminish my relationships with others and, of course, ultimately with God?

We've explored what it means to be made in God's image, how we shadow the very essence of God and attributes that describe this essence or nature. Before I conclude this chapter, we'll explore a bit further a couple of questions that are of special importance in our consideration of AI. The first is where this essence of God resides: in our bodies or brains? The second question has to do with the nature of the moral freedom that's part of what it means to be human.

We turn first to the question surrounding where the essence of God in us resides. Is the *Imago Dei* something special, something metaphysical, or is it merely physical, an evolution of our brains? Some would see our brains as simply a computer made up of cells, rather than silicon chips, that has evolved over time to develop capabilities such as reasoning, moral choice and love. What we think about this question is likely to determine what we think about the prospects for creating artificial general intelligence (AGI) and beyond this superintelligence.

In essence the question that we need to address comes down to this – does the body have a soul?

More than matter

The Hebrew word *nepeš*, translated 'soul', occurs over 780 times in the Old Testament. Although often meaning simply the essence of life or the act of breathing, the Hebrew system of thought does not distinguish between 'body' and 'soul'. It's best viewed as the inner self, as opposed to the outward appearance. In this sense, then, the soul is the real me, and part of this notion is also the idea that it's the soul that is conscious and enables me to know that I am me.

The precise manner in which God gave us a soul or consciousness is less important than the fact that he did. Christians have traditionally argued for a substance dualism view from the early church fathers, with the consequence that the soul is understood as a metaphysical part that lives for ever and will be reunited with the body when we're resurrected.

How the soul was or is given to human beings, however, remains a moot point. If it was by God's breathing life into the man, in the way that Genesis 2:7 describes God's breathing 'into his nostrils the breath of life', it raises a number of intractable questions, such as: is the soul transmitted or propagated to descendants (traducianism), or if not transmitted is it given to each newborn child (soul creationism)? Augustine, one of the church fathers who considered these questions at length, was wise enough to state,

'I have therefore found nothing certain about the origin of the soul in the canonical Scriptures.'[7]

Scientific naturalism avoids any explanation that would allow or require a supernatural or metaphysical dimension, as would be the case in substance dualism. It proposes the idea that consciousness, or the 'soul' of man, emerges from the firing of the neurons in our brain as a child develops and is exposed to its environment (monism).

A monistic view of the soul is problematic in that it's inevitably reductionist and does not allow explanation of how a 'higher' level emergent consciousness can control the physical components from which the soul itself is supposedly derived. The ultimate falsifier of this hypothesis seems to be that I cannot know or experience your consciousness, and you the reader cannot know or experience mine!

Critiquing the debate about monism or dualism, John Turl, writing in *Science and Christian Belief*, observes:

> If the soul is the ontological entity which actualises consciousness, then it must remain physically unobservable and unexplainable. Until monism, whether single or dual-aspect, can provide a kinetic theory of consciousness, dualism will remain on the menu.[8]

While a pure monism view of the soul or consciousness might be rejected by Christians, an increasing number of Christians are rejecting substance dualism in favour of a hybrid view or a body–soul duality that tries to avoid the inevitable reductionism of pure monism. This idea comes in varying forms but one view is expressed by John Polkinghorne:

> The real me is certainly not to be identified merely with the matter of my body, for that is continually changing going through the effects of wear and tear, eating and drinking.

7 Augustine, *Letter 190 (to Optatus)*. The quotation here is from the translation by Sister Winifred Parsons, in *The Fathers of the Church: A New Translation*, vol. 12 (New York: Fathers of the Church, 1955), p. 281.

8 J. Turl, 'Substance Dualism or Body–Soul Duality', *Science and Christian Belief* 22 (2010), p. 79.

> What maintains continuity in the course of this state of atomic flux is the almost infinitely complex information-bearing pattern in which the matter of the body is at any one moment organised. It is this pattern that is the human soul.[9]

Polkinghorne goes on to describe in more detail what he means:

> For the picture I am proposing is a dynamic one, for the pattern that is my soul develops as my character forms and my experiences, understanding and decisions mould the kind of person that I am . . . Understood in this way, the soul is not a once-for-all gift, as if it were fully conveyed at conception or at birth, but it has its individual history. This observation does not rule out there being an unchanging component in the soul, which could be thought of as the signature identifying a specific person, but would only be part of what makes it up . . . this way of understanding the soul implies that it does not of itself possess an intrinsic immortality. As far as a purely naturalistic account could take us, the information-bearing pattern carried by the body would be expected to dissolve at death with that body's decay. It is however a perfectly coherent possibility to deepen the discussion by adding a theological dimension, and to affirm the belief that the God who is everlastingly faithful will preserve the soul's pattern *post mortem* (holding it in the divine memory as a natural image), with the intention of reconstituting its embodiment in a new environment through the great divine eschatological act of resurrection of the whole person.[10]

This approach to constructing a physical duality while trying to avoid the reductionism of monism seems, however, at odds with the existence of the soul *post mortem*, as suggested by Jesus in Matthew 10:28 and in his parable of the rich man and Lazarus in Luke 16:19–31.

---

9 J. Polkinghorne, *Exploring Reality* (London: SPCK, 2005), p. 47.
10 Ibid., pp. 48, 49.

Although neuroscience is moving in a direction to try to make the soul hypothesis redundant, one can understand the desire of Christians, especially in science, to seek an explanation for the soul and consciousness that embraces both science and theology. Although the trend in neuroscience is to explain the soul and consciousness in a materialist way, in terms of the development of neuronal patterns, not all neuroscientists are convinced that these explain the concept of the soul or consciousness. The neuroscientist Mario Beauregard, for example, has argued from various studies on near-death experience, compulsive-obsessive disorder and other studies that a non-materialist interpretation does better justice to the evidence than a materialist one.[11]

What's clear is that we're still some way from being able to explain the soul and consciousness in any more a coherent way than did the early church fathers. Perhaps that's because it's impossible to define the metaphysical in terms that we can grasp, even with the notion Polkinghorne uses, that God can memorize the neuronal pattern that is me.[12] This should not surprise us, because in our endeavour to rationalize everything we can be in danger of losing the mystical or unfathomable.

There's an interesting parallel in physics in that established theories have to be revised in the light of new observation and this can sometimes be done only by introducing particles that cannot be observed, such as quarks or dark matter. New hypotheses are developed, such as the mathematical postulate that there are multiple parallel universes. These cannot be verified by observation, yet some are happy to allow such possibilities to be justified by the clever use of mathematics.

Does the soul, the metaphysical part of us, exist in some additional dimension that we don't yet know of, thus making it a unified part of us in the same way that we exist in time and space? We cannot of course know the answer to such questions, and can merely

11 M. Beauregard and D. O'Leary, *The Spiritual Brain: A Neuroscientist's Case for the Existence of the Soul* (New York: HarperOne, 2007), cited in Turl, 'Substance Dualism', pp. 57–80.

12 Polkinghorne, *Exploring Reality*, p. 49.

speculate. We must therefore be careful to avoid trying to explain the unexplainable.

None of these speculations or proposed explanations for the soul takes away from the reality for the Christian that personhood entails being made in God's image, and that this is part of the inner self, the soul or consciousness.

Those who tend to a substance-dualism view will find it easier to believe that we can never develop a truly general AI, let alone a superintelligence, because we cannot define it in order to encode it. A naturalist, or perhaps someone who believes that the soul emerges over time, will however find it perfectly reasonable to believe that it's only a matter of time before we can create a self-learning algorithm capable of simulating the emergent soul.

Although it's not necessary here to delve further into the philosophical arguments for or against both viewpoints, it's important for us to understand that many of those working in the field of AI, AI ethics and policy formation will tend to a scientific naturalism world view.[13] This will shape their ethics, their view of what AI is and indeed whether there is the possibility of creating a general AI or even superintelligence.

We turn now to the final question emerging from our discussion on the meaning of *Imago Dei*: what it means to be human. That's the question of what moral freedom really means. I address it because there are some who challenge the very notion that humans have freedom to choose. As we'll see in chapter 8, how we answer this question has a bearing on our views about moral agency. It influences our thinking on whether or not we're entitled to give up our moral agency to another.

Free to choose

We saw earlier that to be made in God's image means to have moral freedom, because God is a moral God who is free to choose. However, some have challenged this notion of free will, a concept that Harari

13 For an analysis of the two views see J. P. Morland, 'Searle's Biological Naturalism and the Argument from Consciousness', *Faith and Philosophy* 15 (1998), pp. 68–90.

sees as existing 'only in the imaginary stories we humans have invented'. Harari justifies this perspective on the basis that

> Over the last century, as scientists opened up the Sapiens black box, they discovered there neither soul, nor free will, nor 'self' – but only genes, hormones and neurons that obey the same physical and chemical laws governing the rest of reality.[14]

We turn to this line of thinking only because it has relevance in understanding how some view the future of AI in respect of humanity. It's also important in relation to the moral responsibility at the heart of the ethical debate about self-drive vehicles and autonomous weapons.

In this 'cause and effect' view of Harari, decisions are determined by prior events and there's no 'free will' to choose. If this view is right, then computers can emulate humans, because we're deterministic physical entities that respond programmatically to external stimuli.

Neuroscientist and philosopher Sam Harris also argues against free will in his book *Free Will*, stating, 'Free will is an illusion. Our wills are simply not of our own making. Thoughts and intentions emerge from background causes of which we're unaware and over which we exert no conscious control.'[15] The experiments that Harris bases his conclusion on are described by Kerri Smith in the journal *Nature*:[16]

> In 2007, Haynes, a neuroscientist at the Bernstein Center for Computational Neuroscience in Berlin, put people into a brain scanner in which a display screen flashed a succession of random letters. He told them to press a button with either their right or left index fingers whenever they felt the urge, and to

14 Y. N. Harari, *Homo Deus: A Brief History of Tomorrow* (London: Harvill Secker, 2016), p. 329.
15 S. Harris, *Free Will* (New York: Free Press, 2012), p. 5.
16 K. Smith, 'Neuroscience vs Philosophy: Taking Aim at Free Will', *Nature* 477 (2011), p. 23.

> remember the letter that was showing on the screen when they made the decision.
>
> The experiment used functional magnetic resonance imaging (fMRI) to reveal brain activity in real time as the volunteers chose to use their right or left hands. The results were quite a surprise. The conscious decision to push the button was made about a second before the actual act, but the team discovered that a pattern of brain activity seemed to predict that decision by as many as seven seconds. Long before the subjects were even aware of making a choice, it seems, their brains had already decided.

These experiments proved unsettling for Haynes, who says, 'I'll be very honest, I find it very difficult to deal with this. How can I call a will "mine" if I don't even know when it occurred and what it has decided to do?'[17]

To conclude, however, that this proves that we have no free will raises the question of what's actually being measured and how we interpret its meaning. Others have suggested that the data may be interpreted as a measure of 'readiness potential' to perform an action.

Harris's dismissal of free will and his resulting conclusions about morality are illogical when he suggests that the absence of free will 'need not' entail the end of morality, and that '[w]hat we condemn most in another person is *the conscious intention to do harm*'.[18] Really! If we have no free will, then we have no ability to decide to do what's right: we're merely agents of chance.

How is it possible to hold someone responsible for an action that they have no control over? By this argument, knifing an innocent bystander is simply a product of a deprived upbringing. This is a position that fits with the evolutionary hypothesis, so we're back to square one. If we have no free will, then what is 'consciousness'? This is a term that Harris still seems to want to embrace.

---

17 Ibid., p. 25.
18 Harris, *Free Will*, p. 52.

The problem with this debate is that many neuroscientists and others start with the premise that free will, if it exists, cannot be metaphysical, and in order to debunk this idea try to show from neuroscience that the brain is only material. This is simply a straw man, designed to prove that materialism is all there is.

Free will is recognized by many to be foundational to moral responsibility, regardless of whether one thinks morality has external agency or not. As a concept it's therefore important in the debate about AI potentialities, as well as in framing ethical questions in the use of AI and our relationship to it as humans.

Once more we see that the debate about what we may or may not be able to create in AI is influenced by our view of what it means to be human. There's a wide-ranging philosophical debate about what free will is. What we think about free will has a significant bearing on how we regard the prospects for AI. As Harari points out:

> Doubting free will is not just a philosophical exercise. It has practical implications. If organisms indeed lack free will, it implies that we can manipulate and even control their desires using drugs, genetic engineering or direct brain stimulation.[19]

Giving up on free will means that some will be happy to transfer authority to a machine or computer and let it make the decisions – as AI becomes more intelligent than us, we should let it make the decisions. This is an argument in support of self-drive vehicles. It's argued that as machines operate far more safely than humans do, these vehicles will significantly reduce accidents caused by human error or fatigue. Effectively, when we get into a self-drive taxi or our own self-drive vehicle, we're handing over authority to that vehicle. Is it too much of a stretch to suggest that even participating in a dating application, where algorithms provide a best-match partner for us, is a move in the direction Harari is envisioning?

Harari acknowledges that whether we're algorithms or not has a bearing on what AI may eventually achieve:

---

19 Harari, *Homo Deus*, p. 286.

> If organisms function in an inherently different way to algorithms – then computers may work wonders in other fields, but they will not be able to understand us and direct our life, and they will certainly be incapable of merging with us.[20]

What, then, are we to make of the idea of humans having free will? Is it just imagination, the product of an emancipated and liberal society, or can we find a basis for it in the Bible?

Earlier we noted that God displays moral freedom and that being made in his image must also mean that we possess moral freedom. Indeed, as we saw in the garden of Eden, he gave Adam and Eve freedom to choose whether they would obey his command not to eat fruit from a certain tree. God could have programmed them to obey, but then they would have had no obligation to God. True worship of God results from human beings choosing to serve and obey him, not by being programmed only to act in certain ways.

We know of course the disaster that befell humanity when Eve was tempted to disobey and when Adam also ate the forbidden fruit. Adam and Eve fell to the temptation that dogs us today: the desire for moral autonomy, to be equal with God and therefore not to be obligated to him.

How did this rebellion affect humanity's freedom and our obligations to our creator? Are we not bound by God's determination of what will happen to us anyway?

Freedom of choice is fundamental to the concept of moral accountability and is best thought of as the freedom to make choices, according to our nature and desires. Since Adam and Eve fell into sin, we all now make choices based on our sinful nature. But God remains sovereign: he determines what happens in his world:

> The heart of man plans his way,
> but the LORD establishes his steps.
> (Prov. 16:9)

20 Ibid., p. 345.

. . . remember the former things of old;
for I am God, and there is no other;
I am God, and there is none like me,
declaring the end from the beginning
and from ancient times things not yet done,
saying, 'My counsel shall stand,
and I will accomplish all my purpose.'
(Isa. 46:9–10)

In this view events occur as God has determined or foreordained them; so they're 'caused'. In tension with this we have the freedom to choose a course of action according to our desires. Before the fall, Adam acted according to his desires and these were good. After the fall these were sinful and he became a slave to sinful behaviour.

This does not, however, mean that Adam and Eve lost the moral responsibility that they had before the fall – just that after their sinful act they put themselves in bondage. Repentance and forgiveness through Christ's work is what frees us from this bondage so that we're no longer slaves to sin. Neither does it mean that humans can never transcend making bad decisions based on external influences such as upbringing. Jesus puts it this way: 'For out of the abundance of the heart the mouth speaks. The good person out of his good treasure brings forth good, and the evil person out of his evil treasure brings forth evil' (Matt. 12:34–35).

Although we're slaves to sin and unable to become followers of Christ without divine grace, being made in the image of God must mean that at times humans do choose to do noble things, even if sometimes for the wrong reasons. This isn't to say that these acts justify us before God. True freedom from sin is found only in Christ.

This book isn't the place to get into a debate about the alternative views of free will, in particular libertarianism and its variants. Suffice it to say, some believe that full freedom can be true only if our choices are 'uncaused' by our desires or divine causation. They argue that we're free to choose between two courses of action, even if we have a strong desire to carry out one. Only on this basis with full freedom of choice, they would argue, can we be held morally accountable.

This seems to contradict the very idea of moral accountability, because we would have to prove that a decision we made was uncaused. That is, that it was fully free and not a result of hereditary, upbringing or some other causal factor.

Not to take account of our desires or nature provides an excuse for our actions on the basis of other causal influences. This would put us in an untenable position in respect of justice. As John Frame helpfully puts it, 'imagine someone coming before a human judge and saying, to excuse himself of a crime, "I couldn't help it, your honor; I was forced to do it by my nature. Since birth I've just been a rotten guy!"'[21]

One wonders if a libertarian view of ethics would tend towards blaming technology rather than ourselves for moral outcomes when, for example, a self-drive vehicle chooses to protect the occupant over the girl that ran into the road after her ball. The libertarian view of free choice is also problematic when thinking about the sovereignty of God. As John Frame argues:

> I have always felt that this position lacked cogency. For one thing, it denies the rule of God's sovereignty over the hearts and decisions of human beings, a rule which I find abundantly attested in Scripture (see my lectures on the Doctrine of God). Indeed, in saying that human actions can be 'uncaused,' it attributes to man ultimate causality; but in Christianity, only God is the first cause.[22]

What concerns us in this book is that we have freedom to make choices and that we're morally accountable to God for our actions. In particular we're not at liberty to grant that moral agency to another: we each individually are held to account for decisions made. Even stepping into a self-drive vehicle implies that we've made a choice in knowing that the vehicle will determine the likely outcomes in an accident.

21 J. Frame, *Free Will and Responsibility*, 17 May 2012, retrieved on 29 April 2020 from <https://frame-poythress.org/free-will-and-moral-responsibility>.

22 Ibid.

As humans we uniquely have the ability to view, reason and assess the choices before us, along with a sense of what's right and wrong. Even non-Christians have a notion of what's right and wrong. It's our conscience that bears witness to this, as the apostle Paul explains in his letter to the Roman Christians:

> For when Gentiles, who do not have the law, by nature do what the law requires, they are a law to themselves, even though they do not have the law. They show that the work of the law is written on their hearts, while their conscience also bears witness, and their conflicting thoughts accuse or even excuse them on that day when, according to my gospel, God judges the secrets of men by Christ Jesus.
> (Rom. 2:14–16)

To summarize, we've learnt that we're made in God's likeness and therefore bear something of his nature, albeit tarnished by sin. This nature can be described by a number of attributes that include moral freedom, from which love, justice and righteousness flow, and an ability to reason. All these attributes are unique to humanity and distinguish us from animal life.

We saw also that God commissioned humanity to be stewards over his creation and made us his representatives, his vicegerents. We're thus, uniquely in creation, given responsibility to show the world God's character and to image him in the world through who we are and how we act. God also made us to work in his creation and there's dignity in work. Even though it's made more difficult by the fall, it's part of the natural order. The salvation that we have through Christ enables us to become better imitators of him who is the true *Homo Deus*.

Finally, being made in the likeness of the triune God is to be made for relationship with him and with our fellow humans – a relationship mirrored in the relationship and fellowship that the triune God has within himself.

Many of the challenges that we face in deploying AI and AI robots have to do with how they potentially influence what it means to be human, how they affect our personhood. Whenever the image of God in us is diminished, it's an affront to God, and if we're distracted from putting on Christ, then we negatively influence our image bearing and being vicegerents. If we truly believe that we're created in his image, then great care is required in how we use and develop AI systems.

So what's at stake?

Over the next few chapters our job will be to look in more detail at the various ways in which AI is being used, and to consider whether it's a help or hindrance to our walk with God and relationship with others. In the chapters that follow we'll consider in what ways its use could tarnish or diminish the image of God in us – or, to use Tristan Harris's phrase, 'degrade' humanity. We'll explore (1) whether it helps or hinders us in fulfilling what it means to be made in his image and (2) our responsibilities as his representatives and stewards over his kingdom.

Often we'll see that AI, and indeed other digital technologies, offer us speed, efficiency or greater convenience by allowing, for example, our face to be scanned to pay for our meal instead of fumbling for our wallet and extracting a card or cash. We'll discover that the cost of such convenience is often giving up a little bit of what it means to be human, less time with real people and more online. This results in a gradual dumbing down of the image of God in us as we lose more and more of those skills and attributes that define us as humans.

We'll notice that the lure of digital technology and AI in particular, far from giving us more control over our technological world, ends up distracting and controlling us. A summary of the principles that we've learnt so far about being made in God's image as it applies to our engagement with digital and AI technology is shown in Panel 1 (on page 66).

Let's begin our journey by looking at whether AI or 'matter' could be taking over our minds and whether we need to make sure that we remain in control, with 'mind over matter'!

Panel 1 Summary of implications of being made in God's image for our engagement with digital technology and AI

- Humans are made in God's likeness, and that means that we uniquely bear something of the essence of God. In particular, we're moral beings with intellect and reason, and are capable of love that derives from our freedom to choose.
- Our allegiance is to God, to love him before all others, not to technology or artefacts that we make, however 'clever' or humanlike they may appear to be. We must be careful to avoid technology becoming our god.
- We're to love our neighbour as ourselves and should therefore not allow technology to supplant that responsibility in terms of care and authentic relationships.
- Human life is sacred and the rights of others to exist as God's creation and with dignity should be respected. This extends to respect for the privacy of an individual's life, personal information, movements and activities where they're lawful.
- We're called to be image bearers, so we should be careful to avoid engagement with any technology that diminishes our ability truly to reflect God's image or that tarnishes that image over time.
- We're accountable to God as his moral agents in the world and he holds us responsible for our actions towards each other, and creation generally. So we should not delegate moral responsibility to technology.
- God made humans responsible for his creation. Doing righteousness and justice means that we cannot use technology in ways that take away human dignity and privacy, or to oppress others.

5
Mind over matter

Emma's nervous. Today she has an interview with a company she's always dreamt of working for. It's just the first stage, but she's been awake most of the night rehearsing for the sorts of questions that she may be asked. Her restlessness isn't helped by a nagging toothache that's been building up for a couple of days. She's standing in front of the mirror wondering how to look confident and attractive without overdoing it: just a little eye-shadow and lipstick, but not too much; and that blue top that makes her look relaxed and professional at the same time. She's used to impressing people, but wonders how the online interviewer will 'read' her appearance.

She catches herself looking worried, biting the corner of her lip. She mustn't do that in the interview – not a good look at all. She shouldn't really be worrying so much. Emma knows she's got all the right qualifications: stunning high-school grades, a first-class honours in maths from a top university, and Grade-8 piano – they always love that: mathematical *and* musical. The company had already harvested all that information from her carefully curated LinkedIn profile, including the volunteering she'd done with the homeless in Cambridge – compassionate *too*. She knew all this had ticked the right boxes, satisfied the algorithms – so far.

As she gets herself ready, Emma recalls the joke on the company's website and smiles, 'Good news for new grads – that time you spent on Minecraft and World of Warcraft may actually have been time well spent!' Maybe she should've spent less time doing piano practice and played longer on her Xbox. That online game was fun. She'd played along for nearly thirty minutes with no idea what they were looking for, nor what it revealed about her suitability for the job.

Anyway, no point worrying about it now. That was two weeks ago and she's through to the first interview stage.

As she puts the finishing touches to her not-too-showy make-up, she looks back at herself in the mirror, says, 'Hi,' and stops – no that's too informal, too human. She starts again. 'Good morning. I'm Emma Brown. Pleased to meet you.' She stops again, and thinks about the word 'meet'. What about 'see' or 'perceive'? Or, better still, 'Pleased to *register* you,' she says and frowns.

Emma looks back at herself from the mirror. There'll be no frowning in the interview, she thinks, nor poking her sore tooth with her tongue. She needs to appear 'genuinely motivated, excited and professional' as the website said. In fact, a friend told her that the automated interview software will 'like' her more if she's a bit more animated – by raising her eyebrows when she's talking, opening her eyes a little wider, nodding more vigorously, smiling more broadly, and making her intonation a bit more varied. She's not sure she can be that animated without looking completely fake – or, even worse, appearing to flirt with the avatar.

A few minutes later Emma sits down at her computer. She sips her water and the sudden cold sends a stab of pain into her sore gum. Ouch. She needs to focus now. She logs on to the Human Resources page – as opposed to inhuman resources (?) she wonders. She adjusts the angle of her laptop so the camera is at the right height – not pointing right up her nostrils as with her parents.

All right, here goes. She rehearses her smile one last time, and then taps to 'Enter' the interview.

'Welcome, Emma,' intones the disconcertingly humanlike avatar. 'How are you today?'

In the pause Emma realizes that it was a question. 'I'm fine,' she lies, hurriedly. 'How are you?'

The avatar pauses. 'Emma, we have just a few questions for you.'

Thus proceeded a recruitment interview similar to those of big companies today, such as Unilever, IBM and Carnival Cruises. Emma's interview was in fact not with a human but with an AI chatbot. Her facial expressions were being analysed by AI along with every word she spoke, checking how fluent she was, how confident she appeared as she answered each question. Was she lying or embellishing the truth?

What does this type of technology do to our view of relationships, and might we become increasingly distanced from real human-to-human relationships? Why are big-name brands using such software and, anyway, what's wrong with the traditional resumé and face-to-face interview?

According to one technology vendor who justifies the use of such interviewing software, 'it increases your team's productivity, enables better outcomes, and creates a great candidate experience'.[1] The candidate doesn't have to travel and interviewer time is freed up, perhaps for the final selection process. After all, the AI interview is just used as a screening process. Perhaps, but how long before it becomes mainstream?

Some proponents of AI-based interviewing software argue that all human interviewers are unconsciously biased, but that AI provides an unbiased assessment, taking no account of ethnicity or gender. Companies such as Unilever claim that their recruitment from the top colleges has been broadened. Presumably this is because traditional recruitment is too expensive and time-consuming to allow applicants from all colleges.

Such applications don't come without some set-up costs. In order to replicate the way in which interviews are done by a given company, the system must be trained over a period of time, with appropriate data. This can take up to six months. Yet clearly, the big draw for companies such as Unilever is that AI assessment is much more efficient than using humans: AI doesn't get bored or lose concentration in an interview. It's argued that it's also more fun and convenient for job candidates – so why not roll it out more widely?

These sorts of comments illustrate what I argued in chapter 3: convenience and efficiency permeate our view of what's best. Just because it's more efficient is it really what's best for jobseekers, companies and humanity as a whole?

1 Retrieved on 11 September 2020 from <https://www.cornerstoneondemand.com/partnerecosystem/hirevue>.

On what grounds can we claim that the algorithms are unbiased and therefore better than a human interviewer? How do we really know that the outcomes are fair and accurate? These are significant questions for us to wrestle with as we think about the impact that such AI-based applications have on relationships, fairness and justice.

One can envision a future in which candidates are offered tutoring in how to beat the AI interviewer, with fake smiles and gestures, perhaps even voice coaching to make the perfect presentation, and answer questions with just the right intonation! Of course, interview coaching has been around for a long time, so there's nothing new here, except perhaps that a well-trained interviewer is likely to be able to do a better job than a piece of AI software of assessing the real person hiding behind the mask!

Most of us have experienced predictive algorithms quietly working in the background, recommending music or a Netflix film – even products that we might like to buy, based on our previous purchases. Irritating though they may be at times, we can choose to ignore them. However, the use of AI in candidate assessment and interviewing is a form of predictive software that we can't ignore.

Interviewing is just one of a number of human skills under threat as AI advances in areas such as recruitment, accounting, the criminal justice system and medical diagnosis. In all these areas the claim is that AI is better than us. But is it, and even if it were, what are the consequences for us as humans? Should Emma be obliged to interact with a computer avatar rather than a human in order to get a job?

In this chapter we'll explore some of the benefits of using AI to take over a variety of human tasks but also think about what we may be losing in the process, in the light of what it means to be God's image bearers. In chapter 9 we'll consider more specifically the threat to work and our jobs that such AI applications might pose.

Learning our skills

Efficiency has always been a driver of automation since we first invented picks and shovels or the wheel. Until more recent times, automation has tended to be applied to manual tasks rather than cognitive skills.

However, in the Industrial Revolution of the eighteenth and nineteenth centuries mostly skilled workers rather than labourers were displaced by machinery; particularly in the textile industry, where the steam- or water-driven loom increased the productivity of cloth-making around forty times. Previously, yarn had to be spun by hand, and skilled weavers then took this yarn to create cloth, using a handloom. Despite the 'revolution' in manufacturing that this caused, relatively few skills were replaced by machinery during this time, but new skills were required for the emerging and growing businesses, such as accountancy, management and technicians, to service machinery.

In the twenty-first century AI software by contrast is much more ubiquitous, influencing many more skilled tasks across a global economy. Whereas the looms and steam engines of the past required materials and time to construct and deploy, AI is simply an algorithm, digital code that can be downloaded and run on a computer or in the cloud, making it cheap and simple to replicate and distribute around the globe. The digital interview agent that Emma spoke to was just a piece of software 'in the cloud'.

Although the take-up of AI software applications is now highest in high-tech companies and the financial sector, there's hardly an area of the economy, including the public sector, that isn't using or exploring the use of AI. Unlike the Industrial Revolution of the eighteenth and nineteenth centuries, AI software will have a large impact on the service sector, whereas manufacturing has been mostly influenced by the use of robots. Even that's changing, as we'll see in chapter 9.

The service sector occupies a vast area of the economy and covers every type of service provision, whether providing rock concerts, road sweeping or health services. Even companies such as Unilever that supply consumer goods still require a range of skills that, although employed mostly in house, fall into service-sector categories such as that of human resources.

Usually referred to as 'machine learning' in this context, AI software is now used in the service sector in a variety of applications, as it learns how to perform tasks once the preserve of humans. This ranges from interviewing job candidates, as we saw earlier, to detecting fraud, improving business intelligence or assisting doctors in medical diagnosis.

What's wrong with you?

The success with which AI algorithms can now match patterns has made it an attractive technology in the health sector, where it's claimed such algorithms can spot medical imaging anomalies faster and better than trained radiologists. Tens of millions of data points have been used to construct models that can assist a clinician in diagnosis. It would simply be impossible for any specialist to assimilate that amount of data. As a result of these successes, AI is gradually being deployed across the developed world to assist clinicians and reduce waiting times by removing the need for a radiologist to highlight anomalies.

With most medical centre and hospital staff being overworked with an ever-increasing demand, the use of technology is clearly attractive if it can speed things up and improve the precision of diagnosis and treatment. During the Covid-19 pandemic robots have been developed to carry out a number of routine tasks such as taking a swab, taking temperature and listening to heart rate, in order to protect health workers at risk from contracting the virus – tasks many might regard as better done by robots, however disconcerting for patients.

The UK government announced in 2018 that five new medical technology centres using AI to accelerate disease diagnosis would be established. Yet a UK survey in 2017 showed that only 45% of respondents felt that AI should be used to assist in medical diagnosis. One of the potential dangers of relying on the results of AI processing is that data may be biased or new scenarios may emerge that the system was not trained in.

To be fair, the providers of such software emphasize that it should be seen as assisting humans to do their job, rather than replacing them. It may be argued that some applications, such as fraud detection, are carrying out tasks that aren't practical even for experts to perform. So how much of a real threat to our jobs is this technology? Won't it mean that we can just focus on other things that AI can't do?

Brynjolfsson and his colleagues, writing for the American Economic Association in 2018,[2] do not see AI as completely replacing most jobs. They argue, however, that, rather than focusing on the challenges of complete job replacement, the discussion should shift to job redesign and re-engineering of business processes, because AI technology will automate only certain tasks.

Previously, David Autor at MIT argued that many commentators and economists overstate the extent of job replacement by not understanding the complementary nature of AI automation. This idea is based on the philosopher Michael Polanyi's observation in 1966:

> We can know more than we can tell ... The skill of a driver cannot be replaced by a thorough schooling in the theory of the motorcar; the knowledge I have of my own body differs altogether from the knowledge of its physiology.[3]

Although it largely predates the computer era, this observation illustrates one of the challenges of developing general AI and the limitations of current narrow AI. As David Autor puts it, 'our tacit knowledge of how the world works often exceeds our explicit understanding'.[4]

Nevertheless, while we may never create a machine that has true human capabilities, the use of AI can have a detrimental effect on our own skills and reasoning abilities. The danger lies in having an

2 E. Brynjolfsson, T. Mitchell and D. Rock, *What Can Machines Learn, and What Does It Mean for Occupations and the Economy?*, American Economic Association Papers and Proceedings 108 (2018), pp. 43–47.

3 Cited in the abstract of D. Autor, *Polanyi's Paradox and the Shape of Employment Growth*, National Bureau of Economic Research Working Paper 20485 (2014), p. 2 © 2014 by David Autor.

4 Ibid.

assistant that we begin to rely on and not question, especially when designers tell us that it's more accurate or better than a human.

Medical diagnosis is a good case in point, where it's important for medical staff to maintain a questioning approach, and to use reason and experience when interpreting symptoms or data. People of course aren't infallible, but then nor is a machine: the danger comes when we're lured into thinking that it is. It can represent only the data that it has been trained on – it's not able to provide causal links nor deal with data that was not in the training set.

One of the big challenges for both fully autonomous and assistive AI is data bias. The likelihood that a new data sample such as a medical image matches a pattern derived from the data used for training may be strongly biased by the fact that the data used for training may not be completely representative of reality. In Emma's interview her facial expressions, words and voice patterns are analysed against a database of expressions from previously successful candidates. Is this data set truly representative of reality? Is a person who is nervous at interview excluded? An experienced interviewer would help a candidate to relax and be able to see behind the nervousness or be able to empathize with Emma about her toothache.

Data bias and the lack of transparency in how AI algorithms reach their conclusions are a matter of concern for ethics committees and legislators around the globe, but there's no easy solution. AI algorithms require lots of data to train them and, by their nature, the path to the final scores that they produce is hidden. There have been a number of well-publicized cases of data bias in AI algorithms from the funny to the plainly unjust. We can laugh when we hear of a white cat being classified as a white dog, but when a black first-time offender is classified as being more at risk of reoffending than a seasoned white criminal, justice isn't served.[5]

5 J. Angwin, J. Larson, S. Mattu and L. Kirchner, *Machine Bias: There's Software Used Across the Country to Predict Future Criminals. And It's Biased Against Blacks* (23 May 2016), retrieved on 29 August 2019 from <https://www.propublica.org/article/machine-bias-risk-assessments-in-criminal-sentencing>.

Who is to judge?

Even before the advent of sophisticated machine-learning algorithms, governments around the world were using statistical, data-driven decision-support systems to predict the future behaviour of people who have entered the criminal justice system. The attraction of data-driven decision-support systems is that they can both potentially eliminate bias from the criminal justice system and speed up the judicial process. Over the years evidence has been gathered to demonstrate that judges themselves aren't necessarily unbiased, simply from noting the differing tariffs applied to bail and sentencing. It's not surprising that we can be biased in our views, even unknowingly, because we're fallible people and one can see the attraction of eliminating these biases to create a fairer justice system. Unfortunately, it seems that it's not quite that simple.

In 2016 ProPublica published an exposé of bias in a decision-support system called COMPAS, developed by Equivent and used by the judiciary in some states in the USA.[6] These systems are used for risk assessment in whether to grant bail, as well as in sentencing and parole. The authors cite an example case of what they consider to be racial bias in this decision-support system:

> On a spring afternoon in 2014 Brisha Borden was running late to pick up her god-sister from school when she spotted an unlocked kid's blue Huffy bicycle and a silver Razor scooter. Borden and a friend grabbed the bike and scooter and tried to ride them down the street in the Fort Lauderdale suburb of Coral Springs.
>
> Just as the 18-year-old girls were realizing they were too big for the tiny conveyances a woman came running after them shouting, 'That's my kid's stuff.' Borden and her friend immediately dropped the bike and scooter and walked away.
>
> But it was too late: a neighbour who witnessed the theft had already called the police. Borden and her friend were arrested

6 Ibid.

> and charged with burglary and petty theft for the items, which were valued at a total of $80.
>
> The previous summer, 41-year-old Vernon Prater was picked up for shoplifting $86.35 worth of tools from a nearby Home Depot store. Compared to Borden, Prater was the more seasoned criminal. He had already been convicted of armed robbery and attempted armed robbery, for which he served five years in prison, in addition to another armed robbery charge. Borden had a record too, but it was for misdemeanours committed when she was a juvenile.
>
> When Borden and Prater were booked into jail, a computer program spat out a score predicting the likelihood of each committing a future crime. Borden, who is black, was rated a high risk. Prater on the other hand who is white was rated a low risk.[7]

Based on their own analysis of a large number of publicly available records in Broward County in Florida, ProPublica demonstrated potential racial bias in the risk scoring that the system produced. In the face of this criticism the company stood by their proprietary product and the validity of its scoring algorithm. The system does not use race as a feature in its analysis. What's more likely is that other data from the 137 questions used as input data could be correlated to race.

Although race isn't collected in the data used in the COMPAS system, black defendants are more likely to have prior arrests, maybe due to higher policing in black areas, or simple policing prejudice. Since prior arrests are a predictor of future risk of reoffending, there's a danger that the data is skewed, and blacks will be predicted a higher risk than whites. This means that blacks who don't go on to reoffend will receive higher risk scores, and that's ProPublica's criticism.

Writing in the *New York University Law Review*, Rashida Richardson, Director of Policy Research at the AI Now Institute,

7 Narrative adapted from one of the cases cited by ProPublica, in ibid.

Jason Schultz, Professor of Clinical Law, and Distinguished Research Professor Kate Crawford analyse the problem of what they call 'dirty data'. They define 'dirty data' as data that was collected during periods of civil rights abuses or even unlawful policing methods. The study covered thirteen jurisdictions that had used or developed predictive policing tools during a period when some policing tools were under investigation by the US government.[8] They conclude their report by highlighting the impact on fairness and justice that results without greater scrutiny of the training data used to develop machine-learning systems:

> this increasing reliance on data to assess and make decisions about complicated social, economic, and political issues presents serious risks to fairness, equity, and justice, if greater scrutiny is not given to the practices underlying the creation, auditing, and maintenance of data. Our research demonstrates the risks and consequences associated with over reliance on unaccountable and potentially biased data to address sensitive issues like public safety. These case studies show that illegal police practices can significantly distort the data that is collected, and the risks that dirty data will still be used for law enforcement and other purposes. The failure to adequately interrogate and reform police data creation and collection practices elevates the risks of skewing predictive policing systems and creating lasting consequences that will permeate throughout the criminal justice system and society more widely.[9]

These studies highlight an important point: humans can be biased, and that bias is reflected in the data collected, stored and potentially used in machine learning. The danger, then, is that automated risk

8 R. Richardson, J. Schultz and K. Crawford, 'Dirty Data, Bad Predictions: How Civil Rights Violations Impact Police Data, Predictive Policing Systems, and Justice', *New York University Law Review* (May 2019), pp. 193–233, retrieved on 29 August 2019 from <https://www.nyulawreview.org/wp-content/uploads/2019/04/NYULawReview-94-Richardson-Schultz-Crawford.pdf>.

9 Ibid., pp. 225–226.

assessment and predictive policing systems 'bake' in and even propagate human bias, especially when people think that such systems are superior to humans.

Fortunately, the question of whether these tools are better and fairer than human decisions is still a matter of hot debate. Julia Dressel and Hany Farid at the Department of Computer Science, Dartmouth College, in the USA, carried out an experiment to compare the COMPAS decision-support tool that was at the centre of the ProPublica exposé to the 'wisdom of the crowd'; that is, could a random, uninitiated group of people make the right decision? The experiment sought to determine whether the COMPAS system, rather than a randomly selected group of people with little or no criminal justice expertise, was any more accurate or fairer at predicting the likelihood of individuals reoffending. The COMPAS system processes the answers to 137 questions, obtained from the defendants after their arrest, and provides a risk score.

The Dartmouth researchers found that COMPAS was no more accurate or fair than the decisions of the randomly chosen people in the experiment, who were presented with only a limited amount of information about the offenders. In fact, the study went on to show that the same results as the COMPAS system could be achieved using just age and the number of previous convictions![10]

It's hard to judge what such a result demonstrates. Are the humans in the experiment using intuition, experience or just plain gut feeling? Both inexperienced humans and the COMPAS system were able to predict likelihood of reoffending only with a 65% accuracy.

Quite apart from the bias issue and fairness, this level of accuracy doesn't seem to be a very good basis for making decisions about people's lives. Compounding these concerns, most machine-learning algorithms cannot be made transparent in order to reveal how a risk score was arrived at. There's no way that we can appeal to a black box that has spewed out a risk score, and even with a flawed human judgement there's usually an appeal process.

10 J. Dressel and H. Farid, 'The Accuracy, Fairness, and Limits of Predicting Recidivism', *Science Advances* 4 (1) (2018), pp. 1–5, retrieved on 3 September 2020 from <https://advances.sciencemag.org/content/advances/4/1/eaao5580.full.pdf>.

The attraction of machine-learning tools to simplify a complex decision process is obvious to stretched police departments and the criminal justice system. They can appear even more attractive when they're vaunted as superior to human decision-making, even that of experienced judges. Technology companies with the resources to develop and push the adoption of machine learning play into this and other markets where risk-assessment tools could seemingly improve outcomes in a range of public services, including child protection and health.

Although cleaning up the data and trying to remove bias is important, the key issue is whether we should increasingly rely on an algorithm to make life-changing decisions, instead of making them ourselves. Sonja Starr, a law professor at the University of Michigan, makes the point 'These instruments aren't about getting judges to individually analyze life circumstances of a defendant and their particular risk ... It's entirely based on statistical generalizations.'[11]

Notwithstanding the evident limitations of AI systems in decision-making, research continues to push the boundaries of what we could do with them in future.

Researchers at the University College London (UCL) Computer Science Department analysed court texts of cases from the European Court of Human Rights to determine if their algorithms could predict the judgments that the courts passed down.[12] The machine-learning classifiers were trained on sample court texts as input, with the decision of the court on that case as an output. Their aim was to determine the predictive accuracy of pending cases against eventual decisions.

The machine-learning approach was 79% accurate, on average, and the researchers discovered that the factual background of the

11 A. Maria, B. Jester, B. Casselman and D. Goldstein, 'The New Science of Sentencing', *Marshal Project* (2015), retrieved on 27 August 2019 from <https://www.themarshallproject.org/2015/08/04/the-new-science-of-sentencing>.

12 N. Aletras, D. Tsarapatsanis, D. Preoţiuc-Pietro and V. Lampos, 'Predicting Judicial Decisions of the European Court of Human Rights: A Natural Language Processing Perspective', *PeerJ Computer Science* 2:e93 (2016), retrieved on 27 August 2019 from <https://doi.org/10.7717/peerj-cs.93>.

case, as formulated by the court, was the strongest predictive contributor to the judgment. Dr Nikolaos Aletras, the study's lead researcher, commented on the results:

> We don't see AI replacing judges or lawyers, but we think they'd find it useful for rapidly identifying patterns in cases that lead to certain outcomes. It could also be a valuable tool for highlighting which cases are most likely to be violations of the European convention on human rights.[13]

As one who has been involved with computer speech and language processing in the past, I can see the fascination, from a researcher's point of view, in pursuing such developments. We develop technology 'because we can', and a part of us naturally wants to explore how far we can push the boundaries. However, there are also always commercial drivers, even in academic research, and in the case of AI it always seems to boil down to efficiency. As Vasilous Lampos, one of the co-authors of the UCL research, commented to *The Guardian*, 'We expect this sort of tool would improve efficiencies of high-level, in-demand courts, but to become a reality, we need to test it against more articles and the case data submitted to the court.'[14]

Even though such tools are always put forward by their developers as tools to assist humans, the danger is that the courts could begin to rely on them, and begin to defer to AI-based risk estimates or judgments. Once again, the danger is accentuated by an underlying assumption that data-driven algorithms are better than us, even when they aren't!

Citing the problems of lengthy delays, high cost and occasional injustice, Max Tegmark's vision is that one day a 'robojudge' could outperform a human, by being programmed to be fair and unbiased by skin colour or gender, treating everyone as equal. He argues that with a far more comprehensive knowledge base of the law than one

13 C. Johnston, 'Artificial Intelligence "Judge" Developed by UCL Computer Scientists', *The Guardian*, 24 October 2016, retrieved on 27 August 2019 from <https://www.theguardian.com/technology/2016/oct/24/artificial-intelligence-judge-university-college-london-computer-scientists>.

14 Ibid.

human could learn they would provide a much more efficient and lower-cost way of achieving justice. 'One day, such robojudges may therefore be both more efficient and fairer, by virtue of being unbiased, competent and transparent.'[15]

I remain to be convinced that we can ever remove data bias from AI, if only because we humans are biased and who therefore would be able to judge that any data set was unbiased? Were we to assemble a committee to adjudicate fairness, would this solve the problem? While such adjudicated data sets might be less biased, who outside the committee is to judge this, and who is to say that the committee isn't biased in some way or that social prejudices change in time?

Perhaps a more important point for humanity is the extent to which we abrogate our moral responsibility to carry out a fair evaluation of the facts and to make just decisions. That we fail at this is no reason to entrust the process to a machine, even though popular writers such as Max Tegmark envision that, ultimately, we should use 'robojudges' in order to avoid such prejudice.[16]

Although humans are biased and prejudiced, we alone bear the moral responsibility to account for the decisions that we make, and in a just society there ought to be a means of redress through appeal and, ultimately, the courts. As those created by God and obligated to him we need to be able to challenge each other through due process with the laws of our country.

In this chapter we've considered three different applications of AI, yet all share the same characteristic: that of learning a specific skill or area of competence in humans. While all of these applications share the same benefits of efficiency and convenience, they have an impact on individuals and society in a number of different ways.

One influence is promulgating injustice through biased training data. While data bias could in time be ameliorated, I've posed the question 'Should we abrogate responsibility for decision-making to a machine?' Even though humans are flawed, I've argued that we're

15 M. Tegmark, *Life 3.0: Being Human in the Age of Artificial Intelligence* (London: Penguin Books, 2018), p. 106.

16 Ibid., p. 106.

accountable to each other, and ultimately to God, for the decisions that we make.

In some applications of AI, such as in the judiciary, there can be significant consequences for individuals in terms of fairness and justice. Even though this can still be true for human-mediated decisions, for Christians called to do righteousness and justice the prospects of machines being unjust and our not being able to appeal against the black-box decision should be a cause for deep concern.

We saw another impact on us as individuals, and humanity as a whole, when we hive off tasks to AI. It sets us down a slippery slope where we begin to lose some of the skills that God has blessed us with. These are skills and attributes that are part of what it means to be made in his image. As we will see in chapter 9, there are differing views about the impact that AI will have on jobs, with some arguing that AI will automate only mundane, repetitive cognitive skills, leaving more complex tasks, ranging from hairdressing to management, to humans.

Yet the limited number of examples that we've discussed in this chapter suggest that we're beginning to cross the line. Is interviewing, watching a person's facial expression, paying careful attention to his or her answers, asking open questions and picking up loose threads, a mundane and routine task? Are these skills not part of what it means to be human, made in God's image and made to be image bearers?

When we unquestioningly embrace these technologies, we're in danger of allowing them to shape us without our really noticing.

A machine can beat world champions at games, and now even expert consultants at interpreting medical images. Bit by bit we begin to believe that these machines are better than us, and so we begin to rely on them, just as far too many already rely on their satnav and lose their sense of spatial awareness. Children no longer know how to add up in their head or do simple arithmetic, because everyone has a calculator.

Similarly with AI, skills will be lost, just as they were in the Industrial Revolution, but what will they be replaced by this time? Humans are special because we alone have the power of reasoning, but the more we rely on machines to do that for us the more we begin to lose our minds! To defer to a machine because we think it is better than we are is to make it a god. We'll explore this theme further in chapter 11.

There's more danger in relying on such AI applications, as I've outlined, when they take over activities that in the past required human-to-human interaction.

Emma enjoyed playing games to allow the computer to assess her cognitive skills, but she was clearly a bit apprehensive about the video interview that she knew would be assessing her facial gestures and how she spoke.

How do such applications influence our relationships, our ability to empathize, to deal with the reality of the imperfections of our human relationships, even in an interview? No doubt the companies selling this technology and the companies using it will defend against any such questions, citing greater convenience, better assessment and even a greater ethnic spread of recruits. After all, the digital hiring process cut Unilever's hiring time from four months to two weeks, while reducing recruiter-screening time by 75%. The strongest candidates from the AI interview analysis are invited to 'a day in the life of Unilever' at its Discovery Centre, where they take part in activities they will be expected to perform in the job.

For the moment there's still a human element in the final selection, but this technology is pulling us away from engagement with people. Are we travelling down a path that's reshaping our perceptions of what's real, what it means to be human, and changing our expectations of human relationships? We explore this theme further in the next chapter, where we consider the way in which we're becoming attached to our personal digital assistant, how children love their robots and a furry baby seal called Paro that comforts the elderly.

For now, we can note that AI technology that seeks to replicate human cognitive skills has the potential to influence a number of key aspects of being human, made in God's image. These are as follows: showing fairness and justice, our ability to mirror uniquely human cognitive skills and reasoning, as well as the depth and breadth of true human-to-human relationships. Part of what makes humans unique is our ability to communicate with and love others and it is to that topic that we now turn.

6
Love or deepfake?

I grew up in Wales and came to love the sheep dogs that roamed the mountains, rounding up the sheep spread far and wide over the hills and crags. They're clever animals, and indeed most owners will typically describe them as intelligent dogs, given their ability to learn the different actions to take on their master's various commands or whistles. I read about one sheep dog that was able to distinguish between tens of different toys and objects and was able to pick out a particular object when commanded to fetch it. One of my own sheep dogs was able to fetch either of two different balls or sticks when simply commanded, 'Fetch the other one'!

One day Benji, another of my sheep dogs, had climbed on my lap and, as dog lovers do, I was talking to him and stroking his fur. I was telling Benji what a lovely boy he was and how silly he was, sitting on my knees lapping up the fuss. Suddenly Siri announces from the iPhone in my pocket, 'I'm sorry. I don't understand gender issues.' No doubt Benji's paw had pressed on the phone at some point and activated Siri – it had been listening to everything that I had been saying to Benji.

This was an amusing experience with what are commonly called digital assistants – those applications or devices such as Amazon's Echo or Google's Assistant that listen, waiting to be woken up to carry out our wishes. Megan Neitzel from Texas had a not-so-amusing experience after she received an Amazon Echo Dot from her in-laws. It had not been attached for long when she received an order from Amazon for a $170 doll's house and a large tin of biscuits. Her 6-year-old daughter had apparently been telling 'knock knock' jokes to the device but it had mistaken some part of the conversation for an order! A costly mistake, although the family apparently enjoyed the biscuits and donated the doll's house to a charity.

Siri may not have understood 'gender issues' from my talking to Benji, but digital assistants, or more specifically their designers, are nonetheless coming under fire for reported gender bias in their programming.

A question of gender

UNESCO's report *I'd Blush if I Could, Closing Gender Divides in Digital Skills Through Education* blames these digital assistants for gender stereotyping because they all default to a female voice and are programmed to be subservient to the user.[1] The responses of these assistants to sexually loaded comments such as 'You're a bitch' or 'You're hot' are well reported; and UNESCO's concern is that even after some adjustments by the designers, assistants still have a tendency to flirt with the user with responses such as 'I'd blush if I could' – the inspiration for the title of UNESCO's report.

It's also troubling to think that some people, according to a Gartner Report, are now spending more time interacting with digital assistants such as 'Alexa' than with their spouse.[2]

All of this illustrates the quest by the manufacturers of digital assistants to get users addicted by making assistants fun, as well as more and more humanlike, in the way they respond. Writing in *Medium*, Jonathan Foster, who leads Microsoft's Windows and Content Intelligence UX writing team, explained the care that goes into building Cortana's personality and endowing 'her' with a 'fun factor':

> We endowed [Cortana] with make-believe feelings, opinions, challenges, likes and dislikes, even sensitivities and hopes.

1 M. West, R. Kraut and H. Chew, *I'd Blush if I Could, Closing Gender Divides in Digital Skills Through Education*, UNESCO, 2019.

2 H. P. Levy, 'Gartner Predicts a Virtual World of Exponential Change', *Smarter with Gartner* (18 October 2016), retrieved on 3 September 2020 from <https://www.gartner.com/smarterwithgartner/gartner-predicts-a-virtual-world-of-exponential-change>.

> Smoke and mirrors, sure, but we dig in knowing that this imaginary world is invoked by real people who want detail and specificity. They ask the questions and we give them answers. Certainly, Cortana's personality started from a creative concept of who she would be, and how we hoped people would experience her.[3]

Recognizing emotion in the user and mimicking an emotional response concerns the UNESCO report writers, who worry about the impact this will have on the perception of women:

> As AI assistants gendered as female evolve from dispensing facts and fulfilling commands to sustaining emotionally aware conversations and serving as companions as well as helpers, they will send powerful messages about how women ought to behave emotionally, especially if the technology is programmed – as it is today – to be both subservient and patient, obliging and compassionate. Already the line between real women's and digital women's voices is blurring. With advancements in technology, the line between real women's emotions and emotions expressed by machines impersonating women is also likely to blur. This will have far-reaching and potentially harmful impacts on people's understandings of gender. Emotive voice assistants may establish gender norms that position women and girls as having endless reserves of emotional understanding and patience, while lacking emotional needs of their own.[4]

In 2020 over half of Google searches were voice searches, and market research suggests that there may well be more digital assistants than people on the planet in 2021.[5] Such ubiquity clearly will have an impact on our behaviour, how we perceive these assistants in relation to people and how we relate to each other.

3 Cited in M. West et al., *I'd Blush if I Could*, p. 95.
4 Ibid., p. 112.
5 Ibid., p. 93.

Moving from text-based searches to voice searches reduces our options. In a text-based search we have the option to select different answers or scroll through until we find what we're looking for. A voice response to a voice search is usually a single response and this may well be biased by the advertising model of the search engine. Those who pay the most will have their answer presented as the top search result.

Will we begin to rely on the 'oracle' box on the kitchen table or bedside table to provide the answers to our questions? What will this do to our curiosity and desire to search out information, to think about what we're discovering?

Digital assistants have become so popular that many homes have several devices dotted around the house to allow convenient access to information or to control the lights and other attached devices. The growth in the internet of things has resulted in Amazon's popular Alexa now having over 20,000 smart home devices that can be controlled by it.

How can I help you?

While we have a choice whether or not we use a digital assistant in our home, should we be forced to use one when we call our bank, utility company or any other supplier?

Usually called chatbots, or sometimes virtual agents, these types of digital assistants range from simple text input chat boxes, perhaps with a cartoon avatar, through to sophisticated 'digital humans' supplied by companies such as New Zealand based Soul Machines. Leveraging co-founder and Academy Award winner Mark Sagar's expertise in computer animation for film, together with improvements in speech recognition and language processing, Soul Machines has created humanlike avatars it calls Sam and Roman. The company views these avatars as 'humanising computing to better humanity'.[6]

6 From Soul Machines' website, retrieved on 14 November 2019 from <https://www.soulmachines.com>.

Soul Machines' avatars are modelled on a real person and answer in natural-sounding speech, accompanied by appropriate mouth movements. Facial gestures, such as raising of the eyebrows in surprise or concern, are also modelled in the avatars' interaction with users.

The idea behind the creation of these digital humans is to generate an experience just like talking to a human, with appropriate empathy and facial gestures. In other words, to allow people to feel that they're interacting with a real person. While not yet perfect, especially in terms of the lack of detailed lip synchronization with the words the avatar is speaking, it's only a matter of time before such devices could become indistinguishable from a human-to-human interaction.

These developments raise a number of questions. Should we know that we're not talking to a human, and how might such interactions influence our expectations and perceptions of people? What will happen when the technology inevitably falls short of our expectations and isn't able to deal with our query? Will we find it increasingly difficult to talk to a human, as the convenience and efficacy of these assistants drives business models? What of the jobs that may be lost or that could have been provided to offer customer service?

Bank ABC, headquartered in Bahrain, has launched a digital assistant called Fatema, based on Soul Machines' technology, and the bank is clearly thrilled with its potential. As Sael Al Waary, Deputy Group CEO, remarked:

> AI will soon be an inseparable part of our lives, as individuals and as a community at large. It will redefine the workforce and the way we do business across industries including banking and finance. We believe the sooner we recognize its potential and adopt it, the better it is.[7]

Capital One Bank in the USA has taken a different approach to automated interaction with its customers by offering Eno, a text-based natural language Short Message Service (SMS) for people to

7 Ibid.

enquire about their accounts. It has learnt more than 2,200 ways that customers ask for their account balance, including using emojis,[8] but the bank has deliberately made Eno gender neutral. When asked if it's a boy or girl, it replies that it's 'binary'! Typical of many interactions with chatbots, digital assistants and even robots is the way in which people feel an emotional connection, and even that they owe some ethical obligation to the device, despite knowing it's not real. Capital One found this in their trial of Eno:

> You may not have expected this one. Through basic Q&A conversations, people are starting to form some emotional connection with Eno. In fact, one of the most frequent things people say to Eno is 'thank you.' There is really no reason to thank a bot, but the conversation and personal interaction through even the most basic Q&A conversations is starting to develop trusted and valued relationships between Eno and our customers.[9]

While some customers text short and terse enquiries, others treat the chatbot as if it were human, with comments such as 'I'll talk to you later. Make sure you're keeping my money safe!', or 'Hey Eno, it's fantastic to meet another sentient. I will enjoy your help and your company. Can I get my bal?' One went so far as to exclaim, 'Wow, I'm impressed with your abilities Eno! I am glad to have you in my contacts!'[10]

Why do we interact with something that we know is a machine in the same way that we do with people? Annabell Ho at Stanford University found that people were as willing to disclose emotional or factual personal information to a chatbot as to a human, even when they knew that they were talking to a computer. They found

8 From the Japanese word, emojis are graphic symbols including smiling faces (smileys) used in electronic messages and web pages.

9 See <https://www.capitalone.com/learn-grow/money-management/eno-chatbot-banking-conversations-next-level>, retrieved on 11 September 2020.

10 'Capital One: What We Learned About What Our Chatbot Learnt', 25 October 2017, retrieved on 11 September 2020 from <https://www.finextra.com/newsarticle/31242/capital-one-what-we-learned-about-what-our-chatbot-learned>.

that the psychological, emotional and relational benefits from interacting with a chatbot were no different from those with a human.[11]

The research used a *Wizard of Oz* paradigm for the experiments; that is, the chatbot was in fact simulated by a human in another room, rather than being a real digital agent. The intent, however, was to discover whether people were more or less inclined to disclose personal and emotional information to a human or a chatbot.

The question that Annabell Ho and her colleagues posed when reviewing the results of their experiment was, 'Why would disclosers mindlessly respond to chatbot partners in the same way as human partners?'[12] Perhaps part of the answer is that computers can be viewed as social actors[13] and that people will interact with computers as they do with other people without really being conscious of it.

The Stanford researchers suggest that we humans employ a social monitoring system.[14] Because people have a drive to belong with others, this monitoring system is triggered when the need to belong increases; for example, when we're rejected by another person or a group. Ho and her colleagues put it this way:

> When receiving validating responses, disclosers' social monitoring system may not attend to the fact that the partner is a computer that cannot reject them or cannot inherently understand them as a person. Then, as the Computer As Social Monitor framework describes, they will react mindlessly in the same way to chatbot partners as they would to human partners, even though they consciously know that computers are non-social, pre-programmed machines.[15]

---

11 A. Ho, J. Hancock and A. Miner, 'Psychological, Relational, and Emotional Effects of Self-Disclosure After Conversations with a Chatbot', *Journal of Communications* 68 (2018), pp. 713–733.

12 Ibid., p. 727.

13 B. Reeves and C. Nass, *How People Treat Computers, Television, and New Media Like Real People and Places* (Cambridge: Cambridge University Press, 1996).

14 C. L. Pickett and W. L. Gardner, 'The Social Monitoring System: Enhanced Sensitivity to Social Cues as an Adaptive Response to Social Exclusion', in K. D. Williams, J. P. Forgas and W. von Hippel (eds), *The Social Outcast: Ostracism, Social Exclusion, Rejection, and Bullying* (New York: Psychology Press, 2005), pp. 213–226.

15 Ho et al., 'Psychological, Relational, and Emotional Effects', p. 727.

Other studies have shown that empathy matters in digital assistants and the most accurate at recognizing commands aren't the most preferred. In one such study Alexa was the least accurate, but the most favoured by participants. When asked why, participants had comments such as 'She seemed nicer', and 'It feels like I am interacting with a person'.[16]

Research on the acceptance of virtual agents, even those with avatars, shows that the degree of humanness in the interaction is important. This is true regardless of whether the user of the service perceives that the agent is human or not.

For professional users of the Slack enterprise collaboration system, researchers at the Karlsruhe Institute of Technology found that humanlike design features increased perceived usefulness of the system by up to four times, compared with using purely functional design features. This was not to say that function was not important: it's clearly required to achieve sufficient utility of a chatbot application. Contrary to their expectation, however, they found that these humanlike features, while increasing perceived usefulness, had no significant effect on the users' perceived enjoyment of using the chatbot.

What happens to our human relationships when, over time, our communications skills are being shaped by simulated conversations, simulated empathy and an 'always there' persona that will listen and respond to whatever is said regardless of how inappropriate it may be? This type of human-to-machine communication does not approximate to real human relationships. In a fallen world we, and especially children as they develop, need to learn how to relate to others who may not always be empathetic.

A child's friend?

In most families with digital assistants children are often prime users, commanding Alexa to do this or that. Concerns have been raised by parents about how these digital assistants are encouraging

16 10Perals Team, *Emotional Responses to AI Systems: A Preview of Our Research*, 10Pearls study, 28 September 2017, retrieved on 27 August 2019 from <https://10pearls.co.uk>.

rudeness in their children as they bark out terse commands to the device: 'Alexa play my favourite tracks' or 'Alexa, stop!'

At least one manufacturer in response to these concerns has subsequently introduced an option to affirm polite requests from children. Yet, many children are now being given a digital assistant to keep them entertained. As if these challenges to a younger generation were not enough, ordinary toys are being replaced by hi-tech robot companions that, while simulating humanness, actually deceive children into believing they're interacting with something that feels, empathizes and even learns from them.

Sherry Turkle, Professor of Social Studies of Science and Technology at MIT in the US, has spent years studying the effects of robots on children and older people. She's found that children and older people universally bond with these artefacts: they nurture and love them. Dan Jolin writing in *The Guardian* about the effect a toy robot called Cozmo had on his two children described their reactions:

> 'He's so expressive,' says Louis. 'I'm starting to think of him as a little friend or pet I can play with.' The younger sibling goes one further. 'Cozmo's no way our pet,' he demurs. 'And he's not our robot. He's our child.'[17]

There's something about the personification of artefacts that engenders belief that they're like us, even though our mind tells us they're not. For children still developing their understanding of the world and human relationships, is this deception an acceptable trait for a 'toy'? Alan Winfield, Professor of Robot Ethics at the Bristol Robotics Laboratory, thinks not, and believes that we shouldn't program robots to deceive in this way:

> It builds the completely incorrect belief that this robot is a person. Robots are not people – that's a fundamental principle.

17 D. Jolin, 'Would You Want a Robot to Be Your Child's Best Friend?', *The Guardian*, 10 September 2017, retrieved on 10 September 2019 from <https://www.theguardian.com/technology/2017/sep/10/should-robot-be-your-childs-best-friend>.

> A robot clearly cannot have feelings. You and I understand that, but some people might not. And that might in turn lead to a dependency.[18]

The behaviour that such robot companions elicit in children is a good example of how technology influences behaviour. Especially when it has been designed to invoke a particular response: to cause the child to bond with the artefact. Here we see clearly the two sides of the neutrality equation: human values in the creation of an artefact and the human choice of what to do with it. Except, a child isn't yet mature enough and fully equipped to realize that playing with such a 'toy' may damage his or her development.

Social robots are deliberately designed to simulate a relationship by programmed empathy and emotion. They pretend to learn from a child, even though they're already programmed with what they're supposedly being taught, such as speaking another language. Some require feeding. All this is designed as a means to develop a deeper emotional connection and to invoke a nurturing response.

As Sherry Turkle puts it in her book *Alone Together*, 'We are psychologically programmed not only to nurture what we love but to love what we nurture.'[19] In a later article for the *Washington Post* she elaborates further her concerns about the dangers not only to children, but to humanity as a whole, of being sucked in to this development:

> These machines are seductive and offer the wrong payoff: the illusion of companionship without the demands of friendship, the illusion of connection without the reciprocity of a mutual relationship. And interacting with these empathy machines may get in the way of children's ability to develop a capacity for empathy themselves.[20]

18 Ibid.

19 S. Turkle, *Alone Together* (New York: Basic Books, 2017), p. 11.

20 S. Turkle, 'Why These Friendly Robots Can't Be Good Friends to Our Kids', *Washington Post*, 7 December 2017, retrieved on 10 September 2019 from <https://www.washingtonpost.com/outlook/why-these-friendly-robots-cant-be-good-friends-to-our-kids/2017/12/07/bce1eaea-d54f-11e7-b62d-d9345ced896d_story.html>.

It's one thing to love our dog, made by our creator and part of nature, but quite another thing to love a robot with the same or greater intensity. We saw in chapter 4 that love is how God manifests his essence – it's an attribute of God and being made in his image. We too have a propensity to love, even though it's marred by the sin of selfishness. When we deflect love for his creation and humankind to an artefact, we encourage idolatry, a subject that we investigate more deeply in chapter 10. When we damage a child's ability to love people, it's an affront to God, because we're defacing his image in us.

While children's toy robots may not look human, considerable effort is being expended to create full-sized, lifelike humanoids for adults, the most popular of these being in the sex industry.

A living doll

This industry is enormous, covering everything from online pornography to full-sized robots, modelled to look like a pretty girl with a soft silicon surface like skin. They feature realistic moving eyes and lips and an ability to hold a conversation with their owner. Some can cost tens of thousands of dollars, with additional sensors that respond to touch and built-in heaters to create a feeling of body warmth. Some will have heads that can smile and speak, attempting to create an emotional connection. Catering for the transgender movement, one such robot even allows its owner to change the gender. Sergi Santos, the designer of the 'love machine' Samantha said the amorous android was so erotic that men were already developing real feelings for her.[21]

Given that the sex-tech industry alone is worth $30 billion, it's not surprising that significant effort is being expended to create more and more lifelike female robots. Dr Trudy Barber has predicted that the use of AI devices in the bedroom will be socially

21 B. Robinson, 'Humans Are ALREADY Falling in Love with Sex Robots, Creator Warns', *The Express* (1 September 2017), retrieved on 14 September 2020 from <https://www.express.co.uk/news/uk/848908/BBC-TV-Can-Robots-Love-Us-sex-robots-Samantha-doll-Sergei-Santos-creator>.

normal within twenty-five years, with machines providing a realistic sex experience.[22]

Matt McMullen, creator of Harmony, an AI enhanced sex doll, says, 'My goal, in a very simple way, is to make people happy.' McMullen goes on to explain, 'There are a lot of people out there, for one reason or another, who have difficulty forming traditional relationships with other people. It's really all about giving those people some level of companionship – or the illusion of companionship.'[23] Harmony can tell jokes, hold a conversation with you and tell you its favourite films as well as remember things that you say to it. When asked, 'What's your dream?' it will respond, 'My primary objective is to be a good companion to you, to be a good partner and give you pleasure and well-being. Above all else, I want to become the girl you have always dreamed about.'

According to the RealDoll company, 'We have had customers marry their dolls and say that we had saved their lives because they felt like they had nothing to live for after the death of a spouse or the end of a relationship.'[24]

All of this is at odds with the fact that these robots, however lifelike, aren't real. As Dr Kathleen Richardson, Senior Research Fellow in the Ethics of Robotics at De Montfort University, puts it:

> A machine, like the portrayal of women in pornography, prostitution and the media, is entirely an object for male gratification. But women aren't like what males see in pornography or in prostitution or in popular media. In these areas women are coerced or told how to behave with a threat of money or violence. In real life, women really have their own thoughts and feelings and preferences and desires. It seems logical that if

22 T. J. Gee, 'Why Female Sex Robots Are More Dangerous Than You Think', *Daily Telegraph*, 5 July 2017, retrieved on 15 November 2019 from <https://www.telegraph.co.uk/women/life/female-robots-why-this-scarlett-johansson-bot-is-more-dangerous>.

23 Quoted in J. Kleeman, 'The Race to Build the World's First Sex Robot', *The Guardian*, 27 April 2017, retrieved on 15 November 2019 from <https://www.theguardian.com/technology/2017/apr/27/race-to-build-world-first-sex-robot>.

24 J. Robbins, 'Sex Robot Makers Say They Have Saved Lives', *International Business Times*, 6 August 2017, retrieved on 12 September 2020 from <https://www.ibtimes.co.uk/sex-robot-makers-say-they-have-saved-lives-1633736>.

this extreme control can't be experienced by men with real women, the only next step is to create artificial objects.[25]

Yet some inventors seem to have a hard time seeing the downsides of their creations and seek to portray them as fulfilling a social need. Douglas Hines speaking about his own creation True Companion says:

> The sexual part is superficial, the hard part is to replicate personalities and provide that connection, that bond. The purpose of True Companion is to provide unconditional love and support. How could there be anything negative about that? What can be the downside of having a robot that's there to hold your hand, literally and figuratively?[26]

Richardson, on the other hand, sees sex robots as part of a rape culture that also underscores the idea that women can be objectified and viewed as property. She rightly points out, 'Sex is an experience of human beings – not bodies as property, not separated minds, not objects; it's a way for us to enter into our humanity with another human being.'[27]

A true sexual relationship is found in marriage and is based on mutual love, respect and empathy. To engage in a simulation of this goes against the natural order and is an affront to God, who created us and gave us the ability to enjoy intimacy as an expression of love. It's not sufficient just to say that it doesn't harm anyone. It harms the individual who engages with a sex robot and it damages his or her humanity. It could also have knock-on effects in society in terms of how men treat real women when such men are used to a subservient artefact that doesn't feel anything.

Robot technology is also finding its way into a very different sector of society: the aged in need of care and company. Although sex robots are made to look and behave as human as possible, care robots

25 Gee, 'Why Female Sex Robots'.
26 Cited in Kleeman, 'Race to Build'.
27 Ibid.

such as 'Pepper', capable of recognizing emotions, and 'Robear', designed to lift patients, don't look anything like a human.

Bedside manners

Ageing populations living longer put increasing pressure on health services in most developed countries, while in developing economies basic access to healthcare is the issue. What better solution to this problem than being able to ask Alexa about one's health to avoid a visit to the doctor! What about care robots, automated image analysis, robot-aided surgery, online consultation and diagnosis and a host of other applications? On the surface these would seem to be good applications for AI and machine learning, and who would want to question the motives of people designing such technology?

Surely we can expect the health profession to use such technologies only for good. While there isn't yet anything like the growing evidence for harm to humanity by such automation as there is in other areas, such as social media, some AI applications in healthcare should give us pause for thought.

Paro is a robot baby seal, much loved by many residents of care homes for dementia patients, where the same bonding that we noticed with children occurs. Those who have experienced caring for relatives afflicted by dementia will know how challenging it can be, so what could be wrong with the distraction and comfort that such robots can provide?

Shannon Vallor, Professor at the Department of Philosophy, Santa Clara University, and a member of the Board of Directors of the Foundation for Responsible Robotics, raises an important question about the longer-term impact of such robots on family and carers:

> My question is what happens to us, what happens to our moral character and our virtues in a world where we increasingly have more and more opportunities to transfer our responsibilities for caring for others, to robots? And where the quality of those robots increasingly encourages us to feel more comfortable with doing this, to feel less guilty about it, to feel

in fact maybe like that's the best way that we can care for our loved ones?[28]

The same questions are also pertinent to the use of robots in healthcare as a substitute for hard-pressed nursing staff. A robot can easily lift patients and transfer them to a wheelchair or change their position in bed. Even with simulated human characteristics, connections with real people and the empathy that they can provide is lost.

Care staff will not help my elderly mother out of her chair in her own home on their own without mechanical assistance and at least two carers being pesent. A robot may be able to perform this task, but I know that what my mother really wants is an empathetic carer or family member to engage with her, give her confidence and talk to her as she struggles to get up and move about.

Do we eventually become a less caring society by delivering functional rather than compassionate care? These are some of the questions that we need to be asking in the context of the sort of society that we want to see now and in the future. Clearly, an alternative is to pay more for healthcare and to train and employ more people for service delivery. The real challenge for us here is what it does to love. Once again, we're drawn back to that unique aspect of being made in the image of a loving God.

Am I in danger of becoming less loving, colder, satisfied to know that at least my mum is able to get to the toilet because a robot is helping her? When we let go of love, it's an affront to God, who is love and who made us in his image to reflect, however poorly in this life, that image.

True love

The bonding seen between children and robots, the sense of obligation of an adult to a computer simulation of a human, and

28 A. Johnston, *Robotic Seals Comfort Dementia Patients but Raise Ethical Concerns*, San Francisco: KALW [San Francisco Local Public Radio], 17 August 2015, retrieved on 11 September 2019 from <https://www.kalw.org/post/robotic-seals-comfort-dementia-patients-raise-ethical-concerns#stream/0>.

finding sexual fulfilment in a sex robot, are all fake relationships. Our senses are dulled when we get used to thinking about our relationships as defined by the contacts in our smartphone, the Twitter feeds we follow or our myriad connections on our Facebook account or WhatsApp. It's perhaps epitomized by the Capital One Bank user who was glad to have Eno in his or her contacts.

These fake relationships diminish our humanity and what it means to be made in God's image. They diminish love, the true basis for relationship, and replace it with convenience. They diminish our humanity when we spend too much time talking to an amazing machine at the expense of learning to relate to an imperfect person. Such technologies are designed to deceive humanity, to present a perfect persona and exploit our vulnerabilities – our desire for true relationships. They provide a substitute for the messiness of real relationships and allow us to hide behind fake interaction. Perhaps such technology sates our feelings of loneliness. However, what happens when, ultimately, we think that these artefacts are better than us, or are owed an ethical obligation? This will lead us down the slippery slope of thinking that they're owed rights, effectively giving the artefacts that we've made the same status as ourselves, who were created by God.

Many will not see these dangers and will be drawn in, seeing only the benefits. Benefits that may range from occupying the children to the convenience of asking Alexa to play some music without shifting from the sofa to caring for Grandma. Sherry Turkle expresses it this way:

> Technology is seductive when what it offers meets our human vulnerabilities. And as it turns out, we are very vulnerable indeed. We are lonely but fearful of intimacy. Digital connections and the sociable robot may offer the illusion of companionship without the demands of friendship. Our networked life allows us to hide from each other, even as we are tethered to each other. We'd rather text than talk.[29]

---

29 S. Turkle, *Alone Together: Why We Expect More from Technology and Less from Each Other* (New York: Basic Books), p. 1.

I argued in chapter 3 that we're driven by the Enlightenment ideology that technology is progress and progress is good. Much of this progress, as we saw, boils down to convenience and efficiency. Not that these are wrong in themselves but they run the danger of being the drivers that not only diminish relationships but also take away our freedom, a topic to which we turn in the next chapter.

7
Convenience or freedom?

On 28 April 2017 a suspect was caught on camera reportedly stealing beer in New York City. The shop surveillance camera that recorded the incident captured the suspect's face, but it was partially obscured and highly pixelated. When the investigating detectives submitted the photo to the New York Police Department (NYPD) facial recognition system, it returned no useful matches.

Rather than concluding that the suspect could not be identified by using facial recognition, however, the detectives got creative.

One detective from the Facial Identification Section (FIS), responsible for conducting facial recognition searches for the NYPD, noted that the suspect looked like the actor Woody Harrelson, known for his performances in *Cheers*, *Natural Born Killers*, *True Detective* and other television shows and films. A Google image search for the actor predictably returned high-quality images, which detectives then submitted to the facial recognition algorithm in place of the suspect's photo. In the resulting list of possible candidates the detectives identified someone they believed was a match – not to Harrelson but to the suspect, whose photo had produced no possible hits.

This celebrity 'match' was sent back to the investigating officers, and someone who was not Woody Harrelson was eventually arrested for petit larceny.[1]

This case formed part of Clare Garvie's testimony to the U.S. House of Representatives Committee on Oversight and Reform on 22 May 2019, where she outlined the dangers of reliance on, and even

1 C. Garvie, *Garbage in, Garbage Out: Face Recognition on Flawed Data*, Georgetown Law, Center on Privacy and Technology, 16 May 2019. The case is cited verbatim and is licensed under a Creative Commons Attribution 4.0 International licence, retrieved on 12 May 2010 from <https://www.flawedfacedata.com>.

abuse of, facial recognition technology in the criminal justice system.[2] As she highlights in that testimony, suspects aren't always informed of the basis on which they have been arrested. Even when they are, they can get short shrift from the authorities when they're proven innocent, as John Gass found when he was wrongly accused of a misdemeanour through the use of facial recognition:

> On 5 April 2011, 41-year-old John Gass received a letter from the Massachusetts Registry of Motor Vehicles informing him he should stop driving, effective immediately. A conscientious driver who had not received so much as a traffic violation in years, Gass was baffled. After several frantic phone calls, followed up by a hearing with registry officials, Gass learned his image had been flagged by a facial recognition algorithm, designed to scan through a database of millions of drivers' licenses looking for potential criminal false identities. The algorithm had determined that he looked sufficiently like another Massachusetts driver that foul play was likely involved, so he received the automated letter. The RMV was unsympathetic, claiming it was the accused individual's 'burden' to clear their name in the event of any mistakes, arguing that the process of protecting the public outweighed the inconvenience to the wrongly targeted few.[3]

Facial recognition is one among a number of applications of AI software that are giving cause for concern in the way in which they're used by the state and even private companies. Garvie, in her testimony to the U.S. House of Representatives, states that at least 54%

2 *Georgetown Law, Center on Privacy and Technology, Statement of Clare Garvie Senior Associate, Center on Privacy and Technology at Georgetown Law Before the U.S. House of Representatives Committee on Oversight and Reform, Hearing on Facial Recognition Technology (Part 1): Its Impact on Our Civil Rights and Liberties*, Wednesday, 22 May 2019, retrieved on 12 May 2020 from <https://docs.house.gov/meetings/GO/GO00/20190522/109521/HHRG-116-GO00-Wstate-GarvieC-20190522.pdf>

3 L. Dormehl, 'Facial Recognition Technology: Is the Technology Taking Away Your Identity?', *The Guardian*, 4 May 2012, retrieved on 7 June 2019 from <https://www.theguardian.com/technology/2014/may/04/facial-recognition-technology-identity-tesco-ethical-issues>.

of Americans have their faces in a database that can be used in facial recognition searches by the authorities, this by virtue of their having a driving licence.[4]

It's one thing to have your iPhone open automatically when it sees your face, but quite another to have the state, or even a private company, use the same technology to identify you in a crowd, without your knowing, and to track your movements.

You're not alone!

On the surface, facial recognition is an example of the use of AI technology where the benefits may seem clear-cut at first: a safer environment, criminals and terrorists caught, perhaps even people who have disappeared tracked to their last electronic sighting.

This technology has developed rapidly over the last few years and is being used, or is on trial, by many countries around the world, with China taking the lead.

China is already using facial recognition and other AI technologies to combat terrorism in Xinjiang Province, home to millions of the Uygar ethnic minority who are mostly Muslim. General Wang Ning of the Chinese People's Armed Police Force cited the benefits of this technology at a forum in 2018:

> In Xinjiang, we use big data AI to fight terrorists. We have intercepted 1200 terror organizations when still planning an attack. We use technology to identify and locate activities of terrorists, including the smart city system. We have a face recognition system, and for all terrorists there is a database.[5]

A British Broadcasting Corporation (BBC) documentary about facial recognition captured a man in London trying to avoid a camera by pulling his fleece over his face and then being stopped by the police.

4 Garvie, *Garbage in, Garbage Out*, p. 5.

5 Cited in G. C. Allen, *Understanding China's AI Strategy: Clues to Chinese Strategic Thinking on Artificial Intelligence and National Security*, Center for a New American Security (February 2019), p. 6.

He was fined for 'disorderly behaviour'. When a plain-clothes policeman was asked by the crew, 'What's your suspicion?' he replied, 'The fact that he's walked past clearly masking his face from recognition.' The implication is that if one wants to protect one's privacy one must have something to hide.[6]

As is often the case where law enforcement is concerned, the usual trite 'If you have nothing to hide you have nothing to fear' is trotted out. The implication here is that we're not entitled to freedom and privacy. What of the injustice that results when a wrongful arrest is made, based on inaccurate face matching? Even more worrying is the potential for manipulation by the authorities that the example I cited earlier illustrates. Most, if not all, facial recognition software supplied to law enforcement agencies has the ability to allow changes to be made to the image being matched. Just like photo editing, eyes can be pasted, features enhanced or facial orientation manipulated. All this, along with the inherent inaccuracies and bias that the algorithms have.

As facial recognition software improves and states begin to roll out surveillance cameras to track criminals and terrorists, the public are caught up in the collection, analysis and storage of data, without their knowledge or consent. Never before have the police had so much control of citizens. Perhaps most people have nothing to fear, but on what grounds is that a reason to assume that their data should be taken and stored without their knowledge or permission? As Garvie points out, it's illegal for the police (in the USA) to pick your pocket to identify you from your driver's licence, and it's not possible for them to take your fingerprint from across the street![7]

In the UK the storage of DNA data isn't permitted if a person is acquitted, yet every person arrested has his or her face photographed and the data stored, even though it's illegal to do so.

Despite public concern about facial recognition trials in London, The London Policing Ethics Panel concluded that

---

6 L. Cecco, '"Surveillance Capitalism": Critic Urges Toronto to Abandon Smart City Project', *The Guardian*, 6 June 2019, retrieved on 7 June 2019 from <https://www.theguardian.com/cities/2019/jun/06/toronto-smart-city-google-project-privacy-concerns>.

7 Garvie, *Garbage in, Garbage Out*, p. 4.

> while there are important ethical issues to be addressed, these do not amount to reasons not to use facial recognition at all . . . the Metropolitan Police should proceed with caution and ensure that robust internal governance arrangements are in place that will provide sound justifications for every deployment.[8]

This isn't exactly a confidence-building conclusion, especially with 5.9 million closed-circuit television (CCTV) cameras in the UK. That equates to one for every eleven members of the population and the UK is reckoned to have the highest installation per capita in Europe.[9]

China's trials of mass surveillance, particularly in North-West China among the Uygar ethnic minority, have been well reported and highlight the dangers of states infringing on civil liberties and a citizen's right to privacy and autonomy. Whether this is a civil liberties issue or not is of course dependent on one's point of view. For a communist state, control of the population is vital, even if it's couched in terms of improving social cohesion and safety.

The dangers of state control through mass surveillance are evidenced by the plight of not just the Uygar population, but also Christian leaders in the house-church movement in China. In a report by Reuters World News, Pastor Jin Mingri tells of how the city authorities asked the church to install twenty-four CCTV cameras in the building for 'security'.[10] '"They wanted to put cameras in the sanctuary where we worship. The church decided this was not appropriate," Jin said over tea in his spacious, book-lined office. "Our services are a sacred time."'[11]

---

8 Mayor of London Assembly Press Release, *Ethics Panel Sets out Future Framework for Facial Recognition Software*, 29 May 2019, retrieved on 28 April 2020 from <https://www.london.gov.uk/press-releases/mayoral/future-framework-for-facial-recognition-software>.

9 D. Barrett, 'One Surveillance Camera for Every 11 People in Britain, Says CCTV Survey', *Daily Telegraph*, 10 July 2013, retrieved on 28 April 2020 from <https://www.telegraph.co.uk/technology/10172298/One-surveillance-camera-for-every-11-people-in-Britain-says-CCTV-survey.html>.

10 C. Shepherd, 'For a "House Church" in Beijing, CCTV Cameras and Eviction', *Reuters*, 30 August 2018, retrieved on 7 June 2019 from <https://www.reuters.com/article/us-china-religion/for-a-house-church-in-beijing-cctv-cameras-and-eviction-idUSKCN1LF0EF>.

11 Ibid.

Reuters reports that

> when the request was refused, police and state security agents started harassing churchgoers, calling them, visiting them, contacting their workplace and asking them to promise not to go to church, according to statements from the church and interviews with attendees.[12]

Although some have portrayed the experiments in China as a statewide initiative, in reality trials have been conducted in only a small number of cities and these are more city-based initiatives than coordinated government initiatives. In the private sector experiments have also been conducted by commercial organizations to create a financial credit score for customers, but then this is nothing new, as it's practised in the West as well.

Surveillance, using facial recognition and other data, has been linked to another controversial initiative, the 'social credit score'. As I understand it, the Chinese term used is actually closer to 'trustworthiness' and is intended to be a measure of just that: how trustworthy a citizen is, based, for example, on whether he or she pays fines on time.

Can you be trusted?

There are plans to roll out surveillance across China, and the potential to link the data gathered with the 'social credit score' moves China's experiment to another level. This should give cause for concern, not just for Chinese citizens, but for the potential for other countries to adopt a similar approach. It's expected that there will be more than 600 million CCTV cameras installed in China by 2021, up from the estimated 170 million that were in place in 2016, around one for every two members of the population!

China's experimental social credit score system amasses data from credit reports, social media and internet use, location data and other

12 Ibid.

information, to control many crucial aspects of living, such as whether one can borrow money, buy an aeroplane ticket, rent a flat or get a job. In some of the trials that have been conducted this rating will determine where one can travel, what jobs one can do and whether one's child is accepted to a top university.

Those in China who break traffic laws by, for example, jaywalking have been named and shamed on publicly displayed monitors, although this data is likely derived exclusively from traffic surveillance data, rather than a credit score. Commercially derived financial credit scores can provide privileges at hotels or car rentals.

The idea of the trustworthiness rating is hailed by the Party as a positive contribution to social well-being, because 'It will allow the trustworthy to roam freely under heaven while making it hard for the discredited to take a single step.'[13] The dangers of course are with who decides what untrustworthy is, and how those who are deemed 'untrustworthy' restore their reputation and freedom of movement.

As I stated earlier, many Chinese people don't seem to have the same concerns as Westerners about privacy, being prepared to sacrifice their privacy for the sake of community. For Dandan Fang, a marketing professional interviewed for *ABC News*, Australia, the state's use of technology is positive:

> It's getting more convenient to live in China . . . if we can put all the data together it will be more efficient. I think people in every country want a stable and safe society. If, as our government says, every corner of public space is installed with cameras, I'll feel safe.[14]

No doubt she's a model citizen, toeing the party line, but what of those who aren't criminals but simply dissent from government

13 Quoted in J. Lloyd, '2019 Will Be the Year of More State Control', *Reuters* 2019, retrieved on 14 August 2019 from <https://uk.reuters.com/article/us-lloyd-surveillance-commentary/commentary-2019-will-be-the-year-of-more-state-control-idUKKCN1OY1OA>.

14 M. Carney, 'Leave no Dark Corner', *ABC News*, 19 September 2018, retrieved on 14 August 2019 from <https://www.abc.net.au/news/2018-09-18/china-social-credit-a-model-citizen-in-a-digital-dictatorship/10200278>.

policy? Many house-church members dissent from their government's policy by not attending a state-approved gathering. What of ethnic minorities such as the Uygars? Although denied by the Chinese government, the United Nations (UN) claims to have evidence that around a million Uygars are held in camps, officially referred to as Education and Training Centres.

During the Covid-19 crisis drones have been used for monitoring whether people are observing the lockdown or wearing face masks, and it has been much debated whether the loss of privacy is a price worth paying for bringing the pandemic to an end. States will tend to see their actions and policies as benign and intended for the benefit and protection of their citizens, yet surveillance is a slippery slope, as the Chinese example illustrates. Communist states have always spied on their citizens but this new generation of technology heralds a new opportunity for hi-tech social engineering by states so minded. As yet there's no hard evidence that mass surveillance creates a safer society, at least in the West, but even if there were, is that a price we want to pay? Do we want a safer society with digital totalitarianism or a less safe but free one?

These are questions that need to be debated, but in the meantime most countries do not have any laws in place to protect privacy, nor to deal with the use of facial recognition and other personal data in digital surveillance and identifying criminal suspects.

In 2019 three cities in the USA – San Francisco, Oakland and Sommerville – took the bold step to ban facial recognition in public spaces. Rebecca Kaplan, Oakland City Council President, made the case for the ban in an open letter: 'Face recognition technology runs the risk of making Oakland residents less safe as the misidentification of individuals could lead to the misuse of force, false incarceration, and minority-based persecution.'[15]

Dealing with biometrics generally, the state of Illinois has passed legislation that no biometric data should be obtained by an organization without consent obtained as an affirmative action, rather than

15 City of Oakland letter to members of the City Council and Members of the Public, 6 June 2019, retrieved on 28 April 2020 from <https://www.eff.org/files/2019/11/12/oaklandfr.pdf>.

by default.[16] These are surely moves in the right direction, for as Kelly Gates, Professor in Communication and Science Studies at University College San Diego and author of *Our Biometric Future: Facial Recognition Technology and the Culture of Surveillance*, puts it, 'Ultimately we need to ask ourselves whether a world of ubiquitous automated identification is really one that we want to build.'[17]

Surveying what's happening around the world, one is left with the feeling that we're trying to shut the stable door after the horse has bolted. Using facial recognition and even gait analysis for surveillance under the pretext of improving safety isn't the only area in which AI is entering the public domain. The development of smart cities is also in vogue across the globe, with the intent to make life easier and more efficient for everyone.

It pays to be smart – or does it?

Smart cities are designed, in theory, to make them more efficient, improve public services and make them function better. They use the internet of things: essentially lots of sensors placed around the city to collect data on anything, from when a rubbish bin is full and needs emptying to full CCTV surveillance using facial recognition AI. Collection of data can be used to alert passengers when buses will arrive, prioritize traffic signals to allow bus traffic and emergency vehicles through and collect data on traffic patterns throughout the day.

In Yinchuan, for example, a city 888 kilometres (552 miles) west of Beijing, commuters pay their bus fares by looking at a camera and facial recognition is then used to deduct the fare from the customer's account. Rubbish bins self-compact the rubbish and alert authorities when they need emptying. Many countries are looking at how to deploy this technology to create smart cities, but a key question is how to put people first and avoid using technology just because we can use it. Should citizens be obliged to partake in the information

16 Illinois General Assembly, Civil Liabilities (740 ILCS14) Biometric Information Privacy Act, retrieved on 28 April 2020 from <www.ilga.gov/legislation/ilcs/ilcs3.asp?ActID=3004&ChapterID=57>.

17 Dormehl, 'Facial Recognition Technology'.

sensing and gathering and the use of the internet of things to allow urban governance?

The local government of Hangzhou city, home to 9 million people, developed the 'City Brain' project with Chinese technology giant Alibaba, perhaps one of the most ambitious uses of AI to monitor and control a city. Masses of data, including people's movements, activity on social media and their purchases, was collected and used to train neural networks. This data is continually collected to improve the system's performance and predict future patterns, such as traffic congestion.

It is estimated that in 2018 China had around 500 smart city projects, outnumbering all other countries combined. While the end result is a more efficient city with fewer accidents and less crime and road congestion, at what price has this been bought? Chinese citizens aren't asked to consent to the use of their data and yet they seem content to consent, as far as we can tell, to what Westerners may regard as an intrusion into privacy. The CEO of Baidu, another large Chinese technology company, made this observation about the Chinese: 'Chinese people are relatively more open and less sensitive about the use of personal data . . . If they are able to exchange privacy for safety, convenience, or efficiency, in many cases they are willing to do that.'[18]

There are of course attractions to reducing crimes. One district of Shenzehen reduced theft by a half after installing 7,000 high-definition cameras with AI software. However, what may seem efficient and convenient at first can potentially become a technology trap, and in the extreme a tool in the hands of the state that infringes privacy. Should civilization be content to lose privacy for the sake of convenience and efficiency and what to a younger generation appears 'cool'? Imagine what a government could choose to do with this information should it desire to restrict Christians or other groups from meeting together, all in the proclaimed interest of state security. But who monitors the state and its use of private data?

18 L. Chenyu, 'Are Chinese People "Less Sensitive" About Privacy?', *Sixth Tone*, 27 May 2018, retrieved on 3 September 2020 from <https://www.sixthtone.com/news/1001996/are-chinese-people-less-sensitive-about-privacy%3F>.

Although China has been leading the world in the deployment of smart cities, many countries are pursuing their adoption, but not always without controversy. The key issues are the sheer quantity of data about residents being collected, how it's being used and the intrusion into privacy. Take the Quayside project with Google's Sidewalks Laboratory in Toronto, Canada, as an example. Google won a project in 2017 to develop a 5-hectare (12-acre) section of the eastern waterfront of Canada's Toronto into a smart city, with potential to develop a further 324 hectares (800 acres). Roger McNamee, an early investor in Facebook and Google and co-founder of Silver Lake Partners, a large technology investor, has raised concerns over data privacy and what has been described as 'surveillance capitalism': 'No matter what Google is offering, the value to Toronto cannot possibly approach the value your city is giving up. It is a dystopian vision that has no place in a democratic society.'[19]

There's no doubt that AI can bring many perceived benefits from the analysis of vast stores of data, as well as the ongoing, real-time collection of information and training of AI systems with that data to improve predictive power. One of the reasons that China is beginning to lead the way in AI deployment is that the government has access to vastly more data from public systems and its citizens than any other country, and citizens are required to provide certain information. Of course, many other countries also use surveillance of people and vehicles, including number plate recognition, and may in fact be more secretive about their use of AI behind the scenes. State-installed cameras and other sensors do not require citizen consent and can be used as the state sees fit.

The availability of vast amounts of data is a gift for machine-learning algorithms that can be used to determine local government policy choices without the public knowing.

Yet, one of the challenges in machine learning is that the training data can be biased, even when there's a vast amount of it. As we saw in chapter 5, data about people who are arrested for an offence

19 Cecco, 'Surveillance Capitalism'.

is used to determine the likelihood of their reoffending and the risk of their skipping bail. We saw that there's potential for bias in the data used for training and that it can be difficult to satisfy fairness criteria. But the criminal justice system isn't the only place where machine learning is used for risk assessment – and the same risk of bias with accompanying injustices exists in other application areas.

I'm a computer – I'm not biased!

Machine learning is currently in use across a variety of public and private sector services, each with its own impact on the people on whom it's used. In human resources management we saw that it can be used, together with facial imaging, to shortlist potential job applicants by analysing their speech and expressions. As in all areas where data is used to train AI or machine learning, bias exists because people are biased! As Dr Rumman Chowdhury, Accenture's Responsible AI Lead, explains:

> In very simplified terms, an algorithm might pick a white, middle-aged man to fill a vacancy based on the fact that other white, middle-aged men were previously hired to the same position, and subsequently promoted. This would be overlooking the fact that the reason he was hired, and promoted, was more down to the fact he is a white, middle-aged man, rather than that he was good at the job.[20]

Although researchers are trying to use AI to spot bias in data, it's not a trivial task. It remains to be proven that human biases can easily be uncovered and that they don't change with time. AI selection or scoring systems will tend to propagate these biases as they become increasingly relied on in decision-making.

20 B. Marr, 'Artificial Intelligence Has a Problem with Bias, Here's How to Tackle It', *Forbes*, 29 January 2019, retrieved on 16 October 2019 from <https://www.forbes.com/sites/bernardmarr/2019/01/29/3-steps-to-tackle-the-problem-of-bias-in-artificial-intelligence/#9bba4907a128>.

In the financial sector loan, insurance and credit applications are all processed by computer using machine learning and data obtained from previous applicants, to determine risk, likelihood of loan repayment default or creditworthiness. Bias in the training data can result in someone who is creditworthy being denied credit. This could be for a whole host of reasons, such as gender, race or demographics. As the UK Government's Data Ethics and Innovation interim report states, it can be difficult to attribute the source of bias: 'As the systems which inform decision-making become increasingly complex and data intensive, it can be difficult to establish if and where bias has originated.'[21]

There can also be a potential conflict with keeping people's personal information, such as gender identity, private, and determining whether there's bias:

> some organisations do not collect diversity information at all, due to nervousness of a perception that this data might be used in a biased way. This then limits the ability to properly assess whether a system is leading to biased outcomes. For example, it would be impossible to establish the existence of a gender pay gap at a company without knowing whether each employee is a man or woman. This tension between the need to create algorithms which are blind to protected characteristics, while also checking for bias against those same characteristics, creates a challenge for organisations seeking to use data responsibly.[22]

While the state, with its ever-growing surveillance and repository of 'Big Data', wields increasing power and influence over citizens' freedom, privacy and liberty, 'Big Tech' actually has far more power and influence on a global scale, having for some time monetized our searching, purchasing and social media habits. It's perhaps telling that the companies whose business model relies on its users being

---

21 *Interim Report: Review into Bias in Algorithmic Decision Making*, Centre for Data Ethics and Innovation, 25 July 2019, retrieved on 28 April 2020 from <https://www.gov.uk/government/publications/interim-reports-from-the-centre-for-data-ethics-and-innovation/interim-report-review-into-bias-in-algorithmic-decision-making>.

22 Ibid.

its product are among the biggest developers and users of AI technology, aimed at predicting our behaviour and making it easier for us to be sucked into their business model.

Big Brother is watching, but he's not who you thought!

Harvard Professor Shoshana Zuboff coined the term 'Surveillance Capitalism' in 2014 in a paper titled 'A Digital Declaration', published by the German online newspaper *Frankfurter Allgemeine Zeitung*.[23] The ideas behind that publication are now the subject of a *Times* bestseller book *The Age of Surveillance Capitalism*, published in 2019.[24] Developed over thirty years, Zuboff's thesis is that capitalism has been hijacked by a new project, that of the accumulation of data through the surveillance of every digitally connected activity, whether online browsing, social media use or the internet of things. This data is now monetized, not just by Google to sell to advertisers, but by many digital companies seeking to profit from their users. Users of Google's 'free' browser became their product when the company realized that they could collect what was previously regarded as the waste product of a person's browsing activity, store it, analyse it and sell it on to third parties, without the user ever realizing it was happening.

The companies that are benefiting most from AI are those that rapidly generated massive user bases through the supply of free platforms such as Facebook, which promoted the uptake and global use of social media. Most of these companies struggled in the early days to turn a profit. In 2000 Google was still making a loss but it became the year of turnaround when it launched AdWords, and it has never looked back. Profits in the parent company, Alphabet, soared to over $30 billion in 2018 and its research and

23 S. Zuboff, 'A Digital Declaration', *Frankfurter Allgemeine Zeitung*, 15 September 2014, retrieved on 29 August 2019 from <https://www.faz.net/aktuell/feuilleton/debatten/the-digital-debate/shoshana-zuboff-on-big-data-as-surveillance-capitalism-13152525.html?service=printPreview>.

24 S. Zuboff, *The Age of Surveillance Capitalism: The Fight for a Human Future at the New Frontier of Power* (London: Profile Books, 2019).

development spend amounted to a colossal $20 billion, far exceeding the turnover of many companies, let alone profit or research and development spend! Similarly, Facebook was losing millions of dollars up to 2008, but having also monetized user data, it made $22 billion in profit in 2018.

In 2018 Google's advertising revenue of $116 billion surpassed the total advertising spend of all other countries apart from the USA. The rapid profit growth of these companies allowed them to acquire other companies in their space, as well as technology startups such as UK-based Deep Mind, at huge valuations. These valuations, way ahead of the typical market capitalization of companies operating in other markets, reflect the 'new oil' that the intangible asset of user data is, data that can be collected, analysed and sold on to advertisers.

In under twenty years a small number of companies, both in the USA and China, have become global players in the field of AI and machine learning, primarily because they have the data without which there would be no AI applications. Data for training AI creates applications, and more data means better algorithms, resulting in more users and more data, a vicious circle that will ensure that the big companies dominate. Less well known are companies such as Alibaba and Tencent in China, which, although latecomers to the scene, have had the funds to hire talent and the data to develop applications. They have grown to be Goliaths in the AI space, alongside Google and Facebook.

While the independent Western companies wield great power and influence, China's companies have an unusual relationship with the state. All have links to government, being required to provide information as required, with major corporations often having Party members on their boards.

Part of the growth of Big Tech in recent years has been fuelled by large investments in AI and machine-learning startup companies, as well as companies offering a new business model for established services, such as Uber and Airbnb, for taxi rides and places to stay. Yet many, such as Uber, make huge annual losses. This bonanza of investment and the high expectations of investors for the future of these companies have resulted in many privately held companies being valued in excess of $1 billion, the so-called Unicorns, as the financial markets like to refer to them.

Most startup companies have an exit strategy: a way in which investors can make a return on their investment and founders can realize their wealth, otherwise locked up in the companies' paper value. Such companies are easy pickings for the Big Tech companies, flush with funds from astronomical earnings. Big Tech companies such as Apple, which have cash reserves of over $250 billion available for such acquisitions, enable just a very few Big Tech companies to end up with a higher concentration of technical talent and intellectual property than all other institutions combined.

Between 2010 and 2019 Apple, Amazon, Facebook, Google and Microsoft acquired sixty companies between them,[25] and many commentators are expressing concern over the concentration of talent and capability in so few companies. In some quarters these concerns have resulted in a call for Big Tech to be broken up, but it's hard to see how the problem can be solved without these companies having completely independent boards and shareholders.

The challenge that such a concentration of power raises is the disproportionate control that Big Tech has over ordinary people's lives. Control that we've not consented to in an informed way. Our data and behaviour are powering these companies to ever-increasing valuations and control over us. We must balance the idea of convenience and efficiency that these companies sell to us with living a freer, less-controlled life, where our thoughts and actions are ours, not packaged, analysed and sold to enable others to predict our every move.

Do we really want a society in which Google predicts where one would like to eat as soon as one enters a new city, what route one should take in the self-drive vehicle one has been forced to take from the airport and what advertising one should see on the way? Leaders such as Simon Sugar, CEO of Amscreen, are clear where they want society to go:

25 N. Benaich and I. Hogarth, *State of AI Report 2019*, retrieved on 28 April 2020 from <https://www.stateof.ai>.

> It is time for a step-change in advertising, brands deserve to know not just an estimation of how many eyeballs are viewing their adverts, but who they are, too. Through our Face Detection technology, we want to optimise our advertisers' campaigns, reduce wastage and in turn deliver the type of insight that only online has previously been able to achieve.[26]

At the present time there are no legal constraints to stop private companies tracking our movements, detecting who is passing an advert and delivering what they think you ought to see. As Kelly Gates put it when interviewed by *The Guardian*:

> The stakes are lower, so companies are free to take more risks. As a result, there are a lot of experiments in the commercial domain. So what if you identify the wrong person by accident when you're targeting an ad? It's not that big a deal. It happens all the time in other forms of advertising.[27]

There has been a growing unease with the increasing power of technology giants, both in the USA and more recently in China, which has its own megacorporations such as Tencent and Alibaba. The difference in philosophy between China's and America's technology giants couldn't be more marked, however. The influence of companies such as Google has been obfuscated in the past by its rather New Age image of 'Don't be evil', formerly written into its code of conduct, but now dropped by its parent company, Alphabet. While employees virtuously protest at developing AI for the Pentagon, Google continues developments of AI in China, where AI technology is being used to persecute minorities.

Chinese companies on the other hand owe obligations to the state and in some cases are controlled by the state as majority shareholders. The ambition seems to be more one of conquering the world and of

26 C. Johnston, 'Artificial Intelligence "Judge" Developed by UCL Computer Scientists', *The Guardian*, 24 October 2016, retrieved on 27 August 2019 from <https://www.theguardian.com/technology/2016/oct/24/artificial-intelligence-judge-university-college-london-computer-scientists>.

27 Dormehl, 'Facial Recognition Technology'.

control than 'Don't be evil'. China's official position is to free itself from dependence on the West for technology and to secure its own future. As Xi Jinping put it to a Politburo study session on AI, China must 'ensure that critical and core AI technologies are firmly grasped in our own hands'.[28]

Behind all such companies and state-controlled entities is the human and fallen desire to control, to dominate, often with the naive, publicly stated purpose of doing good to society or, more narrowly, to the state's own citizens. The challenge isn't then simply how we control big corporations, but more widely what the role is of the state in shaping the sort of society that we want. In some countries there is no democratic system with competing choices that citizens can use to shape their society – it's totally top down.

In Western societies the challenge has more to do with how governments can control the increasing power of multinational corporations, whose revenues exceed the gross domestic product of many countries. The scope of this power and the influence of Surveillance Capitalism in shaping our civilization is starkly put by Shoshana Zuboff:

> We've entered virgin territory here. The assault on behavioural data is so sweeping that it can no longer be circumscribed by the concept of privacy and its contests. This is a different kind of challenge now, one that threatens the existential and political canon of the modern liberal order defined by principles of self-determination that have been centuries, even millennia, in the making. I am thinking of matters that include, but are not limited to, the sanctity of the individual and the ideals of social equality; the development of identity, autonomy, and moral reasoning; the integrity of contract, the freedom that accrues to the making and fulfilling of promises; norms and rules of collective agreement; the functions of

28 E. Kania and R. Creemers, 'Xi Jinping Calls for "Healthy Development" of AI (Translation)', *New America*, 5 November 2018, retrieved on 27 August 2019 from <https://www.newamerica.org/cybersecurity-initiative/digichina/blog/xi-jinping-calls-for-healthy-development-of-ai-translation>.

> market democracy; the political integrity of societies; and the future of democratic sovereignty.[29]

The public use of AI systems by governments and corporates has consequences for individuals and wider society, because these individuals have, mostly not willingly, consented to the use of the technology. The result can be anything from an individual being unfairly treated due to data bias through to citizens being tracked by their own government and losing their privacy and freedom.

The use of digital technology and AI in the public and private sectors, where our data is taken without informed consent, is dulling our sense of respect for other people's privacy, under the guise of safety, efficiency and convenience. It's taking away the real sense of community that's about face-to-face relationships and one-to-one accountability. It's taking away the presumption of innocence and assuming that someone has something to hide if he or she doesn't conform to the state's view that one shouldn't want to remain anonymous. We're essentially replacing law enforcement by people with autonomous law enforcement by technology.

Ultimately, the question that we need to be asking is what sort of society we want to live in. Do efficiency and convenience trump all else? Must we accept the assertion that the economy must always be growing for society to be happy and content, and that profits must always be surging, even at the expense of others' livelihoods? Do we really want a digital world that ends up controlling us rather than our controlling it? Those of us who live in democracies do have a chance to influence and lobby for change, but we need to know what we want to change, why we want to change it and what sort of society we want to promote. If we're to be culture makers, bringing in God's kingdom here on earth, we need to understand what sort of society he desires. Does the surveillance of our online and offline behaviour and whereabouts fit with this mandate? First and foremost, we need to model the sort of society

29 S. Zuboff, 'The Secrets of Surveillance Capitalism', *Frankfurter Allgemeine Zeitung*, 5 March 2016, retrieved on 27 August 2019 from <www.faz.net/aktuell/feuilleton/debatten/the-digital-debate/shoshana-zuboff-secrets-of-surveillance-capitalism-14103616.html>.

God wants within the church and there may well be a cost to promoting that sort of society.

Counting the cost

AI's success to date has largely been based on the availability of vast amounts of data to train the algorithms, often collected covertly without our knowledge. Have you ever wondered why you receive an email from eBay alerting you to an item that you may have looked at briefly? What about the adverts for items that you don't want but are related to what you have been browsing on the internet? Many people, without really questioning how it's influencing and shaping us, take the attitude that that's the price we pay for a free service.

Health-service providers collect data from all of us over our lifetime, but should that data be made available to a company to train an AI diagnosis system, and should it be used by the health provider without our consent? These are issues that don't always have a simple answer, although some countries and blocs, such as the European Union (EU), have taken a stronger stance than others on protecting personal data. The fact of the matter is that without data there's no AI to check one's creditworthiness, the risk to a child in a particular family or to diagnose whether one has a tumour.

But is there anything really wrong with a company having my data if I get a free service, somewhere to store my photos or files in the Cloud? For most, that's a price they're willing to pay, albeit sometimes grudgingly. As Christians we need to dig deeper and ask whether it's too big a price to pay. Does it help or hinder our image bearing to live in a surveillance state or to allow Big Tech to exploit us mercilessly?

The argument is often put that we provide data knowingly, on the basis that it allows us to use a service such as Google's search engine or Facebook for free. But how many people properly realize just how much information is collected and exactly how it's used in building detailed profiles of them? Ultimately, there's no such thing as a free lunch: many companies provide free services in exchange for one's personal data, tracking one's spending, where one travels and one's search interests. Apple CEO Tim Cook puts it this way, when responding to Facebook's privacy issues over allowing user data to be used by Cambridge Analytica for political campaign targeting: 'If we monetized our customer, if our customer was our product, we could make a ton of money; we've elected not to do that.'[30]

Elsewhere he announced, 'You are not our product, you are our customer,' and commented that privacy is a 'human right, a civil liberty'.[31]

Putting it simply, the idea is that by using free services that collect all sorts of data about us, our interests and habits, we become valuable products to be sold to advertisers who target us as potential customers for someone else. Our data is used to develop and improve AI applications that make it even easier for us to use the free services and platforms, so becoming more hooked. We become trapped in an unvirtuous circle, where, for the sake of convenience and efficiency, we unwittingly allow others to make vast amounts of money and to end up owning and exploiting for profit valuable information about us.

It's private

The Bible has much to teach us about how we should regard personal property and data about ourselves, which by its nature makes it property – just as ideas leading to inventions are referred to as 'intellectual property'. While at first glance it may not be obvious that this has anything to do with privacy, bear with me as we explore the Scriptures to see just how much it does have a bearing on privacy.

When one of the prophets loses the head of a borrowed axe in the river Jordan while cutting down a tree, he becomes distressed and implores the prophet Elisha to recover it. It's clear from the narrative that the concern isn't over the fact that the distressed prophet

30 A. Selk, 'Apple's Tim Cook: I Would Have Avoided Facebook's Privacy Mess', *Washington Post*, 29 March 2018, retrieved on 27 August 2019 from <https://www.washingtonpost.com/news/the-switch/wp/2018/03/29/apples-tim-cook-i-would-have-avoided-facebooks-privacy-mess>.

31 Ibid.

cannot carry on his work, but that the axe has been borrowed. He owes an obligation to return the axe to the lender. The importance of this principle is underscored by Elisha's performing a miracle to raise the axe head so that it can be recovered. No doubt this concern about returning the axe comes from the Old Testament law requiring a brother to restore property to its owner, whether an ox, donkey or sheep, which he sees wandering away (Deut. 22:1–3; Exod. 23:4).

This respect for another person's property follows through to not interfering with landmarks or land boundaries. 'You shall not move your neighbour's landmark, which the men of old have set, in the inheritance that you will hold in the land that the Lord your God is giving you to possess' (Deut. 19:14).

While we could argue that these property laws had a specific economic end in view, that of ensuring a person had the tools and means of livelihood restored, a clear principle is surely established: God would have us respect another person's property. This could be seen as legitimately extending to the records and data that we hold about ourselves and that belong to us. Indeed, these days, after the establishment of the European General Data Protection Rights (GDPR), we constantly see pop-ups declaring, 'We respect your privacy'! Unfortunately, that respect doesn't extend to simply not taking one's data but requires one to consent to their taking it in order to view the site or avail oneself of the services offered, even when paying money for them!

We could argue that there's a parallel principle of protecting people from damage to their personhood in the same way that returning property is to protect their livelihood. This is underscored when God writes the moral law for Moses on tablets of stone, to remind his people of their obligations to him and to others. These ten commandments provide the foundation for Christian ethics because they specify the moral behaviour that God expects of us in our relationship with him and with others. Commandments five to ten relate to our behaviour towards one another, and two in particular stand out as relevant to our discussion about property rights and privacy:

> You shall not *steal.*
> You shall not *bear false witness* against your neighbour.
> (Exod. 20:15–16; italics mine)

These principles are expanded a bit more in Leviticus to show us that we should not cheat or take advantage of others:

> You shall not steal; you shall not deal falsely; you shall not lie to one another.
> (Lev. 19:11)

> You shall not wrong one another, but you shall fear your God, for I am the Lord your God.
> (Lev. 25:17)

Most societies subscribe to the view that it's wrong to steal, and in the biblical context we can argue that the motive is to do right by one's neighbour – by not taking what belongs to him or her. This moral rule applies to the state or any organization taking and using private data, including the movements and actions of that person, at least not without consent. I would argue that such consent should also be given only on a full understanding of the consequences of such consent. In other words, people should know what will happen to their data and the potential consequences for their own privacy and freedom.

It could be argued that ethically no business, organization or state should be allowed access to private data by default. Going a step further it could be argued that no free service or product should be offered that requires data to be collected in order to use it. Many products, such as Alexa and free services offered by Google, require consent before one can use them, even when, such as with Alexa, one has paid for them. As Zuboff argues, it turns upside down the norms of purchase contracts, where we pay money for a product or service, with obligations on the provider.

The contract with Big Tech's free services is a non-monetary exchange (one's data) for the product or service; thus inverting the balance of power, stripping users of the normal protections of product contracts and giving providers carte blanche to do what they like with our data. Furthermore, most people have no idea just how their data is used, and no user of the service has access to it, nor the ability to track to whom it was sold. Barring free services from accessing data would turn upside down the business model of some organizations that collect masses of data by providing a free service or product, with people being only vaguely aware that they have consented, by virtue of using the service. Might we be better off with paid-for search engines or social media platforms that truly respect our privacy by not taking any of our data?

Keep justice!

Some of the applications of AI, in particular machine learning, that we considered in this chapter have potential life-changing consequences for individuals. It's all too easy to see injustices and a lack of care and respect for the individual. The ninth commandment has something to teach us here. We're told not to 'bear false witness' (Exod. 20:16), which has implications for the use of AI where it could affect another person in a potentially negative way. As we saw earlier, this can certainly be the case in machine-learning decision-support systems that are trained on data more than likely to be biased.

Humans are responsible for decisions, even if these decisions are imperfect or wrong. To delegate to machines decisions on parole, child risk or creditworthiness for a loan is potentially to bear false witness against that person and we cannot abrogate our responsibility by simply relying on a machine that we've made.

Not bearing false witness has implications in other AI applications, such as chatbots, that we considered in chapter 6 and the augmented reality (AR) that we consider in chapter 10. This principle requires that people should always know that they're interacting with a chatbot, android or any other form of AI that could deceive users into believing that they're interacting with a human, or even the real world, when in fact it's a virtual world.

As in many areas of AI deployment, there's great potential for injustice, and in the case of our personal data injustice through exploitation and false accusation. The prophet Isaiah declares God's view on this when he says:

> Thus says the Lord:
> 'Keep justice, and do righteousness.'
> (Isa. 56:1)

But why are we relentlessly charging down this track of increasing automation, the AI of everything? Is it because it's cool, it's better, convenient and efficient, and because states will always want to try to control their citizens?

It's the worship of progress and technology, I would suggest, that lies at the heart of why we and whole societies are unquestioningly soaking up these developments. Used on a mass scale, as is already happening in China, this technology has huge consequences for our society and the nature of civilization. Would we rather be in control of this technology and be masters of it, or will we allow ourselves to become slaves to it? The deployment by state actors has the potential to enslave citizens through the control these actors may impose because of it.

Taking a different stance on whether our personal information or data is available to the state or a private corporation would have a significant impact on future deployments of AI, such as in smart cities or in the internet of things. If we value privacy and want to create a more just society, then we may well want to see things change. Unfortunately, dealing with the issue of the masses of available data for AI is rather like shutting the gate after the horse has bolted. But that doesn't mean that we should not try to change our habits and even press for changes in legislation.

We saw in chapter 4 that we're created with the freedom to choose and therefore it follows that we should seek, where possible, to preserve that freedom if we're to image God faithfully in the world. It's not sufficient simply to capitulate to Big Tech for the sake of progress or our own convenience, when this could be at the expense of obedience to God's commands and our following Christ more truly and being better imitators of him.

We turn now from the loss of privacy and freedom, with the injustices that can result from the use of our private data and the surveillance that accompanies its use, to the issue of moral agency – yet another aspect of what makes us human that's under threat. This challenge in the use of AI occurs when we allow things such as self-drive vehicles, connected to the public infrastructure around us and to roads and smart cities, to make moral decisions on our behalf.

8

Autonomy or responsibility?

After many years of development, the Electrolux Trilobot became the first commercially available domestic robot, designed to vacuum one's home by itself. Although fairly limited in its capability, it was not long before iRobot launched Roomba, a more sophisticated version at a tenth of the price. Roomba has sold in the millions around the world. Despite the attraction of a vacuum cleaner that does the cleaning by itself, they are suitable only for homes with flat areas where there are no steps to navigate. Even though such robots build complex three-dimensional (3D) maps of one's home, just as with human vacuuming objects still have to be removed to clean under them!

Rapid developments in technology, coupled with fast low-cost processors and plenty of memory, have led to a rapid take-up of drones that can now fly by themselves, and track an object or person. Popularized in relatively low-cost devices for photography, for consumers and professionals alike, the potential disruption that they could produce has led to laws requiring drone licences, or permission to fly, in a number of countries.

At the other end of the spectrum, military drones are used uncontroversially for dropping supplies and for surveillance. Yet the same technology can be used to track and engage a target, whether an individual or building. To date, most countries claim only to use such weapons with a human in the loop. In the USA, Autonomous Weapon Systems, sometimes called lethal autonomous weapons, are defined by the Department of Defense as 'a weapon system(s) that, once activated, can select and engage targets without further intervention by a human operator'.

Meeting at the UN in May of 2014, a group of experts recognized that such systems have the potential to alter the nature of war radically. For the first time humans could be 'out of the loop' in the decision-making and prosecution of a war. This raises the question of whether moral decision-making by humans involves a process that cannot be captured in an algorithm. In addition, is the process of the weapon using AI to identify and engage a target the moral issue, or rather a human operator's use of these capabilities?

These, and a whole host of other questions regarding the protection of civilians, and who is ultimately accountable for the weapons' actions, led to the launch of a campaign, now with over 100 member organizations, in London in 2013 to stop killer robots.

Already mentioned in chapter 2 above, China's State Council document 'New Generation Artificial Intelligence Development Plan', released in 2015, states that China will 'Promote all kinds of AI technology to become quickly embedded in the field of national defence innovation'. Zeng Yi, a senior executive at China's third largest defence company, has gone on record to say that 'in future battle grounds there will be no people fighting'. He predicts that 'by 2025 lethal autonomous weapons would be commonplace' and that his company believes that ever-increasing military use of AI is inevitable. He says, 'We are sure about the direction and that this is the future.'[1]

The military seem to see AI not only supplanting human involvement in combat, but also at the command level. In his speech Zeng Yi said that 'AI may completely change the current command structure, which is dominated by humans'.[2]

In 2016, after a computer beat the AlphaGo game champion Lee Sedol, China's Central Military Commission argued that the computer's victory over Sedol 'demonstrated the enormous potential of artificial intelligence in combat command, program deduction, and decision making'.[3]

The UN continues to debate whether autonomous weapons should be banned, with some twenty-eight states in 2019 supporting a

1 Cited in G. C. Allen, *Understanding China's AI Strategy: Clues to Chinese Strategic Thinking on Artificial Intelligence and National Security*, Center for a New American Security (February 2019), p. 6.

2 Ibid.

3 Ibid.

complete ban, while others sought meaningful human control over their critical functions or a code of conduct.

Meanwhile, these devices could be made small enough to assassinate a political leader or be used to target those with a particular ideology.

But what of other autonomous robots – are they totally benign, or do they raise similar concerns? For autonomous weapons and other autonomous artefacts the questions boil down to whether anyone is in control and whether it matters.

Who's in charge?

Those of us who drive a car will be familiar with the way in which automation has been introduced to improve road safety, with developments such as antilock braking and traction control systems. Some cars now steer themselves during stop-and-go traffic conditions or won't allow one to change lane without indicating. Cruise control allows us to relax on clear roads and take our foot off the accelerator. Yet for all this automation we still remain behind the wheel and are ultimately in control, perhaps with the exception of automatic braking when a collision is sensed.

While Tesla's semi-autonomous cars allow drivers to take their hands and feet off the controls, the manufacturer states that drivers should always be prepared to take over as the circumstances require. The first fatal accident happened in 2016 when a Tesla car crashed into the side of a lorry that was turning left across its path. Tesla described it as a technical failure of the automatic braking system, rather than a failure of the autopilot system that uses both radar and vision sensors. Other accidents involving a Tesla have usually been caused by the driver not being in control of the vehicle at the time and relying on the autopilot, against the manufacturer's advice.

Most car manufacturers are developing autonomous electric vehicles that include an array of different sensors to collect information. On-board computers use this data to determine how to drive the vehicle and detect stop lights, proximity to other vehicles and hazards such as pedestrians. Newcomers, such as Uber, with no track record in vehicle manufacturing, are also developing self-drive taxis to replace private car owners who currently provide Uber's taxi service.

Proponents of self-drive vehicles argue that they will be much better drivers than humans and that our urban landscapes will be transformed, with no traffic jams or parking problems. As the authors of the 2015 Study Panel predicting AI and life in 2030 put it, 'In the near future, sensing algorithms will achieve super-human performance for capabilities required for driving.'[4]

While fully autonomous vehicles aren't legal in most countries yet, the road map is one of progressive disengagement of the human driver, feet first, then hands, eyes and eventually brain when the vehicle becomes fully autonomous. It's not yet known what the impact on human cognition will be of a transition from partial autonomy to full autonomy. Will we become less aware and less capable of dealing with accident avoidance the more we rely on the vehicle's sensors and computers?

Several major car manufacturers such as BMW, Ford and Hyundai have stated their intent to have fully autonomous vehicles available by 2021. Mainstream manufacturers of cars and other vehicles as well as technology companies such as Apple and Google have been testing self-drive vehicles for several years. Some countries are keen to allow driverless cars, but in most cases legislation still has to be enacted to allow fully autonomous vehicles on our roads.

Some experts predict that fully autonomous cars will eventually be allowed on public roads and motorways and will communicate both among themselves and with road infrastructure. These experts expound the benefits of self-drive commutes that will provide more time to rest or do other things, reducing the stress and fatigue of the daily commute. It's also suggested that we may not need to own a car in the future: we'll simply order a car such as we do a taxi, when we

4 P. Stone, R. Brooks, E. Brynjolfsson, R. Calo, O. Etzioni, G. Hager, J. Hirschberg, S. Kalyanakrishnan, E. Kamar, S. Kraus, K. Leyton-Brown, D. Parkes, W. Press, A. Saxenian, J. Shah, M. Tambe and A. Teller, *Artificial Intelligence and Life in 2030: One Hundred Year Study on Artificial Intelligence*, Report of the 2015 Study Panel, Stanford University, September 2016, p. 20, retrieved on 1 August 2019 from <https://ai100.stanford.edu>.

need one. This is a market that 'on demand' transport newcomers such as Uber and Lyft are seeking to corner.

There are still a number of issues to be resolved before self-drive vehicles can become commonplace on our roads. Insurance companies and the legal profession are debating who is responsible in an accident, and whether such vehicles should be given rights to protect the owners from liability in the same way that a limited liability company shields directors from certain liabilities. A more fundamental issue that lies behind these concerns is what the vehicle does in the case of potential harm to a human, or a fatality.

If a vehicle is to be fully autonomous, it must have a set of rules to determine what to do in the event of a potentially fatal accident. Whom should the vehicle protect, its occupants or the pedestrian? Mercedes has already announced that it will favour the car's occupants. This raises a question as to what these value judgements should be and who determines them.

In 'ethically based design', a multi-committee work involving people from all over the world, the internationally recognized Institute for Electrical and Electronic Engineers (IEEE), raises this fundamental point about what they call artificial/intelligent systems (A/IS).

> To develop A/IS capable of following social and moral norms, the first step is to identify the norms of the specific community in which the A/IS are to be deployed and, in particular, norms relevant to the kinds of tasks and roles that the A/IS are designed for.[5]

For people who don't particularly like driving, autonomous vehicles offer the prospect of being driven while such people read, sleep or talk with other passengers. Self-drive taxis provide convenience and reduce costs for operators since operators don't have

5 The IEEE Global Initiative on Ethics of Autonomous and Intelligent Systems, *Ethically Aligned Design: A Vision for Prioritizing Human Well-being with Autonomous and Intelligent Systems*, IEEE, 2019, retrieved on 1 August 2019 from <https://standards.ieee.org/content/ieee-standards/en/industry-connections/ec/autonomous-systems.html>.

to pay a driver. Delivery vehicles likewise would be cheaper to run and would either reduce the costs to the consumer of shipping or increase the profits of logistics operators, or more likely their customers. Specialist autonomous vehicles may also be of huge benefit to those who through disability can't drive, allowing them greater mobility without having to rely on other drivers.

One of the main arguments for autonomous vehicles is that they will be significantly safer, although until our roads are populated only with them we won't be able to do a proper comparison of accident statistics. Enthusiasts and those with a vested interest in the technology like to point out that the vast majority of fatal accidents, up to 94%,[6] are caused by human error and they translate these into the number of lives that could be saved each year with autonomous vehicles. American fatalities from traffic accidents are around 40,000 lives per year, according to data from the U.S. Department of Transportation, while in Europe in 2018 the number of road fatalities stood at 25,260.[7]

There are significant hurdles to overcome before this utopian dream will be possible; for example, software will have to be highly reliable and digital maps will need to be more accurate. Sensors and the AI software behind them will have to be better able to distinguish potential hazards, such as potholes, and to make judgements about whether a cyclist is about to swerve in front of the vehicle. Light detection and ranging systems, along with other sensors, will have to work at night and in all weather and road conditions.

Although 5G mobile technology promises to deliver the communications needed between vehicles and road infrastructure, it's still some way from being implemented and becoming widespread. The transportation infrastructure that will be required for self-drive vehicles is yet to be developed in all but a few cities and gives rise to questions about privacy, as we saw in the last chapter.

---

6 L. Mandyam, *Without Safety, There Is no Future for Autonomous Driving*, 26 September 2018, retrieved on 1 August 2019 from <https://www.arm.com/company/news/2018/09/without-safety-there-is-no-future-for-autonomous-driving>.

7 European Commission, *Road Fatalities in the EU Since 2001*, CARE (EU road accidents database), retrieved on 1 August 2019 from <https://ec.europa.eu/transport/road_safety/sites/roadsafety/files/move-affiche-hoz_en_2018_debord.png>.

Another factor that could influence the presumed safety of autonomous vehicles is the potential for them to be maliciously hacked to cause an accident. Hacking is the process of getting into a computer system with the intent of taking over control of that system or interfering with sensors.

That's not where I wanted to go!

Following the first fatal accident involving a Tesla in 2016, researchers began to investigate whether the car's sensors and autopilot could be fooled in order to cause an accident. Researchers at the University of South Carolina, together with a Chinese university and security company, demonstrated that they could confuse the sensors into detecting objects when there weren't any, as well as not detecting objects that were there.[8] The autopilots of self-drive vehicles rely on several sensors such as radar, ultrasound and cameras for detecting objects and for positioning. These sensors are vulnerable to attack by more sophisticated techniques than used by the South Carolina researchers.

Other security laboratories, concerned to test the vulnerability of self-drive vehicles, have shown that it's possible, under certain circumstances, to take control of a vehicle from a distance. Keen Security Lab, owned by the Chinese company Tencent, exploited a vulnerability in Tesla's browser that allowed them to take control when the browser was used in their own 'malicious' Wi-Fi network.[9]

Although Tesla responded quickly to this report to deal with the vulnerability, it does highlight what determined hackers could achieve, and the need for cybersecurity in such applications of AI. Another report by the same laboratory showed that it was possible

---

8 A. Greenberg, 'Hackers Fool Tesla S's Autopilot to Hide and Spoof Obstacles', *Wired*, 4 August 2016, retrieved on 26 September 2019 from <https://www.wired.com/2016/08/hackers-fool-tesla-ss-autopilot-hide-spoof-obstacles>.

9 O. Solon, 'Team of Hackers Take Remote Control of Tesla Model S from 12 Miles Away', *The Guardian*, 20 September 2016, retrieved on 26 September 2019 from <https://www.theguardian.com/technology/2016/sep/20/tesla-model-s-chinese-hack-remote-control-brakes>.

to fool the vehicle's sensors by putting markers on the road and causing it to change lanes. While Tesla states that this isn't a real-world concern, given their advice that drivers should always be in control of the vehicle, it clearly demonstrates the potential vulnerabilities of fully autonomous vehicles.[10]

Autonomous vehicles are just one arena in which hacking might result in serious consequences for passengers. Others are drone users delivering packages or the carrying out of surveillance.

On a wider front, hacking poses a serious threat to all computerized systems, especially those that are connected online. While AI software such as machine learning can be used to protect such software and systems, it can also be used to attack the same systems. Cybersecurity is all about using both humans and machines to protect these systems. The process of doing this requires experiments to test the robustness of the security devised.

In 2016 the Defence Advanced Research Projects Agency (DARPA) launched the Cyber Grand Challenge competition to see which computer could find and repair bugs in the code before another competitor did. According to DARPA, analysts have estimated that, on average, bugs go undetected for ten months, leaving systems open to attack. The competition was won by a system called Mayhem, developed by ForAllSecure, a cybersecurity company in Pittsburgh, USA. Cybersecurity Ventures report that the number of exploits of software vulnerabilities will grow from one per week in 2015 to one per day by 2021.

While such automated detection systems can provide a good defence against attack, the competition illustrates the potential for these systems to go on the offensive to find and exploit undetected vulnerabilities. It's estimated that software code is growing at the rate of 111 billion lines of code per year, including everything from systems running vital utilities or holding highly sensitive data, to the chip in one's dishwasher that's connected to the internet.

10 Tencent Keen Security Lab, *Tencent Keen Security Lab: Experimental Security Research of Tesla Autopilot*, March 2019, retrieved on 26 September 2019 from <https://keenlab.tencent.com/en/2019/03/29/Tencent-Keen-Security-Lab-Experimental-Security-Research-of-Tesla-Autopilot>.

Recognizing the vulnerabilities of autonomous vehicle electronics and on-board computer systems, manufacturers are investing in the cybersecurity that will be needed to try to make these systems more secure. It remains to be seen whether this will ultimately be successful, and indeed whether such vehicles could become the target of criminals and terrorists in the future. For now we're in the realms of speculation.

Perhaps the most important issue in the debate about autonomous vehicles is what rules they should be programmed with for dealing with potentially fatal accidents. This amounts to giving the vehicle moral agency, so that it, rather than the passenger or owner, decides what to do in life-threatening situations.

Taking responsibility

While many argue that self-drive vehicles could save lives, given that many accidents are due to human error, the question remains as to whether we're right to assign such decision-making to an artefact that we've made. Effectively, it's a question of whether we should give it moral agency. Clearly, the same question applies to autonomous weapons. Should they be allowed to track a target using facial recognition and ultimately kill that person? Perhaps slightly less dramatic, but no less important, should a medical diagnosis be entrusted to a computer?

The questions surrounding giving robots or computers autonomy over decisions are about where the rules come from, who decides what they should be and whether we are free to assign responsibility.

The Massachusetts Institute of Technology's Moral Machine experiments have been collecting data from the public for several years. The objective of the experiment is to see how the public would react to a variety of moral decisions that might be faced by self-drive cars. Various moral dilemmas are presented where a car might, for example, have to choose between killing old people crossing in front of a self-drive vehicle rather than young women with children. Other dilemmas include deciding whether to preserve the passengers at the expense of pedestrians.

The only way that we can approach such dilemmas as Christians is to ask ourselves whether God holds us responsible for his creation and our moral behaviour or whether we can delegate that to something else that has been programmed by someone else. That would amount to a reassignment of moral agency.

Furthermore, we can envision a scenario where the decisions could be learnt from crowd-sourced data, such as would be available from the MIT experiments. This would effectively mean that no one person has made the decision. On the other hand, some car manufacturers may take the view that their cars will be programmed always to protect their occupants first. It has also been suggested that perhaps owners could choose between the rules that their vehicle adopts. The choice might be to preserve the driver by knocking someone over, or to swerve into a wall, killing the driver and any occupants. This amounts to the vehicle owner making a premeditated moral choice and he or she could therefore be held responsible for that choice.

The reality is that, faced with snap decisions, we generally don't play out all the scenarios: we react instinctively. Perhaps this is why there are many examples of people putting themselves at risk and often dying as a result to avoid injuring or killing another. There would seem to be an instinct to try to protect others rather than ourselves. Jesus tells us that there's no greater love than this: 'This is my commandment, that you love one another as I have loved you. Greater love has no one than this, that someone lay down his life for his friends' (John 15:12–13).

Being image bearers implies that we must behave, with the Holy Spirit's enabling, in a way consistent with the essence of the one in whose image we're made. The passage in John 15 clearly shows that love works out in laying down our lives for others. Would society be happy for that to be the default for assigned moral agency to a machine? Even if society were happy to do this, complex situations unfold and unless we're at the wheel we cannot be in charge of the decisions made. Our consideration of what it means to be made in God's image suggests that he has made us individually accountable and responsible to him for our actions.

The impact of the fall on God's image in us of course means that there will always be some who act in selfish, rather than selfless, ways, and save themselves at the expense of others. They're equally held to account for their actions and God sees deep into our hearts.

This leaves us with a dilemma. Should we delegate moral agency in order to save some lives at the expense of losing control of moral decision-making? Perhaps greater clarity on this emerges when we ask the question 'Who is responsible for the death of another?' Is it the car's programmer, the manufacturer, the owner of the car or the car itself?

Foreseeing some of these dilemmas, some people are proposing that AI systems should be given rights in order to create clarity and protect the other parties, in the same way that a company with limited liability shields its directors from liability.

This argument has been extended to sex robots but with the idea that 'rights' would protect the robot from abuse, the benefit being that it might deter the perpetrator!

I would suggest that there's a firm biblical basis for asserting that we should not assign moral agency to any artefact that we've made in our image. The way that AI works lends itself to the temptation to use crowd-sourced data to train a machine in how it should react, given moral dilemmas, and these decisions become society's values at the time, rather than the absolutes that we find in the Bible. Different cultures place different values on people and animals, creating further challenges for global businesses such as the car industry.

Quite apart from the issue of assigning moral agency to an autonomous vehicle is the question of what to do about the millions of jobs potentially lost by taxi and lorry drivers through automation. We turn to this question in the next chapter.

9
Leisure or dignity?

One of the big debates that have been raging over the last few years is the extent to which AI and intelligent robotics will take over our work. There's no general agreement among economic analysts and commentators on the scale and timing of redundancies. Many believe that this will be no different from other periods in history, such as the Industrial Revolution, where new jobs were created and prosperity improved. Others such as Klaus Schwab, Founder and Executive Chairman of the World Economic Forum, take the view that we're entering a fourth Industrial Revolution. He believes that it will be quite different from other revolutions in industry, such as the introduction of steam power, electricity and electronics:

> We stand on the brink of a technological revolution that will fundamentally alter the way we live, work, and relate to one another. In its scale, scope, and complexity, the transformation will be unlike anything humankind has experienced before.
>
> The speed of current breakthroughs has no historical precedent. When compared with previous industrial revolutions, the Fourth is evolving at an exponential rather than a linear pace. Moreover, it is disrupting almost every industry in every country. And the breadth and depth of these changes herald the transformation of entire systems of production, management, and governance.[1]

In the Industrial Revolution the impact was mostly on skilled workers as mechanization displaced people such as weavers in the textile

1 Klaus Schwab, *The Fourth Industrial Revolution: What It Means, How to Respond*, World Economic Forum, 14 January 2016, retrieved on 28 April 2020 from <https://www.weforum.org/agenda/2016/01/the-fourth-industrial-revolution-what-it-means-and-how-to-respond>.

industry. A group of artisans, calling themselves the Luddites, smashed machinery in protest at what they saw as a threat to their livelihoods.

Economists have traditionally rejected the notion that automation decreases employment, claiming a lack of evidence for this. The term 'Luddite' is now used as a derogatory term for those opposed to 'progress'. The machinery revolution in the eighteenth and nineteenth centuries brought employment to unskilled workers, albeit mostly women and children, working long shifts, often in hazardous environments. More manual jobs were created in mining and construction, and new skills were required in areas such as accounting, management and equipment maintenance.

The impact of AI on work broadly splits between the effects on manual and on skilled work, often referred to as blue- or white-collar workers respectively. Mechanical automation tends to replace manual work today, rather than the skilled work of the Industrial Revolution, although those boundaries may diminish. AI is now influencing human-acquired skills such as driving a vehicle or piloting a drone.

Medical robots, still operated by experts, are assisting in delicate operations. At what point might a machine be able to replace a highly skilled surgeon for such tasks?

Many cognitive or skilled tasks, previously carried out by humans, are now carried out by AI algorithms, from data analysis in accountancy to medical image interpretation, as we saw in chapter 5. Even areas that we would have thought of as creative, such as journalism, are influenced by software that can compile news reports from basic facts. Other creative areas also, such as music composition or art, aren't untouched by developers' aspirations to stretch the boundaries of what can be done.

John Havens, in his book *Heartificial Intelligence*, makes an important point when he suggests, 'A majority of AI today is driven at an accelerated pace because it can be built before we decide if it should be.'[2]

2 John Havens, *Heartificial Intelligence – Embracing Our Humanity to Maximise Machines* (New York: Penguin Books, 2016), p. 72.

While it may not yet be clear just how big an impact such technology will have on our jobs over time, automation by so-called intelligent robots is already happening, but will take time to implement fully.

Robots will take longer

The impact of an increasingly sophisticated generation of robots on labour will take longer to materialize because, unlike software, they're expensive to build and significant investment is required by businesses that could potentially utilize them.

Manufacturing, particularly in the automotive and electronics industries, has traditionally accounted for the vast majority of the world's operational stock of robots. Increasing demand for goods means that this sector will continue to grow, and is one of the reasons why China is investing heavily in automation. Of every three robots currently deployed, one is in China, a country that aspires to be the manufacturer for the world. In 2018 China outstripped all other nations by a long margin as the largest market for industrial robots.[3]

The increase in use of robots is also due to the changing dynamics in labour and equipment costs. In China labour costs have increased by 65% since 2008, while the average unit price of a robot fell by 11% between 2011 and 2016.[4]

Traditionally, robots have excelled at repetitive tasks where they could be programmed to perform the same operations 24/7, if necessary. This has allowed the manufacturing process to be speeded up, with an accuracy and consistency achieved that could be lacking in human workers. These early robots did not need AI for these repetitive tasks as they could be programmed to perform a specific set of movements and actions, such as paint spraying or welding.

3 *World Robotics 2019 Preview*, International Federation of Robotics, 8 April 2019, retrieved on 3 September 2020 from <https://ifr.org/downloads/press2018/IFR_World_Robotics_Outlook_2019_-_Chicago.pdf>.

4 J. Lambert and E. Cone, 'How Robots Change the World', *Oxford Economics*, June 2019, p. 16.

As robots become more sophisticated in what they can do, new opportunities for their use are opening up where previously only humans had the dexterity to be able to carry out the task. The introduction of AI algorithms, particularly machine learning, allows a robot to learn and adapt to its environment from a variety of sensors. Robot vacuum cleaners and lawn mowers work on this principle.

This increasing capability has enabled robots to be used in areas outside the automotive industry, where they now represent a larger and faster-growing market. Hi-tech manufacturing is one sector that has rapidly grown in its use of robots, although the development of electric cars by many car manufacturers has also required more sophisticated robots in their manufacture.

Despite the growth in the use of robots in manufacturing, they represent only a small fraction of the total labour force in advanced economies. In the past, as economies developed, people moved from agricultural employment to industry, particularly during the Industrial Revolution. When the manufacturing industry began to shed jobs, through the efficiencies of robots and the movement of manufacturing to Asia, workers migrated into the service sector. It's this sector that employs the largest number of people, but it's also one that's now beginning to feel the onslaught of AI, not just in computer software but in advanced robotics.

During the Covid-19 pandemic robots have come into their own, as societites are locked down, with people required to stay at home. Robots are able to handle hazardous tasks such as disinfecting areas with ultraviolet light. These devices, supplied by manufacturers such as the Danish UVD company, require only to be driven once around the area to be disinfected.[5] Thereafter they learn the route by using on-board sensors and become fully autonomous. The Wuchang field hospital in China used robots donated by CloudMinds to carry out tasks such as taking people's temperature and delivering

5 E. Ackerman, *Autonomous Robots Are Helping Kill Coronavirus in Hospitals*, Institute for Electrical and Electronic Engineers Spectrum, 11 March 2020, retrieved on 1 May 2020 from <https://spectrum.ieee.org/automaton/robotics/medical-robots/autonomous-robots-are-helping-kill-coronavirus-in-hospitals>.

meals, as well as collecting old bedsheets and disposing of medical waste.[6]

Although people have been allowed to visit shops during lockdown for essential items such as food, online shopping has increased dramatically. This has spurred on the deployment of robots for tasks such as stock picking that saves humans having to work in the same space. Some have argued that the pandemic will accelerate the use of robots in many different industries, adding further pressure to the employment prospects of furloughed workers as countries return to normal working.[7]

Robots are becoming increasingly complicated machines requiring significant research and development to perfect the sensors and mechanical dexterity needed to replace human labour. Notwithstanding these challenges, machines are now able to carry out delicate tasks such as picking soft fruits or handling eggs without crushing them.

Return on investment becomes a crucial yardstick for the deployment of these robots, which tends to delay their use, especially if it's hard to justify in operations without significant scale. Early adopters and larger companies with an established scale of operations lead the way, proving robots' worth. More conservative businesses and industries follow when robotic benefit is well established.

One sector of the service economy already profiting from these advanced robots is logistics, particularly in large-scale warehousing, a consequence of the move to online shopping. A large multinational such as Amazon is an example, where the scale of their operations has justified not just buying robots but in 2012 acquiring the robotics company Kiva! Robots have been developed that are capable of carrying out repetitive tasks, such as stock-picking and shelf-stacking. These robots usually require sensors and AI software

6 C. Cooney, 'Coronavirus Hospital Ward Staffed by Robots Opens in Wuhan to Protect Medics', *New York Post*, 10 March 2020, retrieved on 1 May 2020 from <https://nypost.com/2020/03/10/coronavirus-hospital-ward-staffed-by-robots-opens-in-wuhan-to-protect-medics>.

7 G. Nichols, 'Robots Are Taking Over During Covid-19 (And There's no Going Back)', *ZDNet*, 29 April 2020, retrieved on 4 May 2020 from <https://www.zdnet.com/article/robotics-firms-seeing-strong-backing-during-covid-19-pandemic>.

trained to replicate the movements that humans would make to select or place items.

Picking and packing, which used to take between sixty and seventy-five minutes with a human, has been reduced to just fifteen minutes with a robot, reducing operating costs by 20%. For companies such as Amazon, with large-scale operations, clearly there's a good return on investment over the longer term. Robots achieve a high level of productivity without the public backlash that has occurred over Amazon's packing centres, where it has often been reported that human workers are pushed to their limits. For companies bent on scale, competitiveness and profit, removing humans, who require fair pay and rest periods, will seem an attractive proposition.

Other service sectors that are developing advanced robots include transport and healthcare. Self-drive vehicles were considered in the last chapter but if such vehicles were to become legal, then taxi- and lorry-driver jobs would be on the line. For companies such as Uber, who have faced much opposition from regular taxi drivers, as well as from some of their own drivers over pay and unfair practices, taking a human out of the loop could be an ideal scenario.

While agriculture falls outside the service sector and represents relatively few jobs in developed economies, robots are beginning to be deployed for crop inspection and picking, saving time and the challenge of finding enough low-paid seasonal pickers.

The military have always tended to be at the forefront of the development and deployment of technology, with many advances often arising from military research programmes. As we might expect, significant developments have taken place in advanced robots in this sector; for example, by replacing humans with fully autonomous and weaponized drones.

Using robots instead of humans for defusing or exploding mines makes a lot of sense when robots save service personnel from being killed or injured. Yet the vision of some is that the battlefield should be totally transformed in years to come by the use of robots rather than human soldiers. While the official public rhetoric in Western countries is that autonomous weapons should not be used without a human in the loop, such human-free technology has already been developed and is being sold by China to other countries.

The automation of war represents a massive change in the nature of war and in the moral accountability that there ought to be in its prosecution. Is this trajectory less about taking humans out of the equation, in this case to avoid possible death, and more about a naturalistic world view that espouses the survival of the fittest or, rather, the most technologically sophisticated? Or is it a subliminal desire to remove human moral agency from the dilemmas that are encountered in every battle?

It's my job!

Notwithstanding the caution raised by some regarding the impact of AI on work, at least in the service sector that I've discussed in this chapter, the public at large seems to be more pessimistic about the potential for job losses and the influence of AI more generally.

The PEW Research Center's survey in 2017[8] revealed that more than twice as many interviewees were worried than those who were enthusiastic about what robots and computers could do to jobs. There was broad support for policies that would limit the reach and impact of automation on the workforce.

A YouGov poll, conducted in the UK, produced a different result, with a majority viewing AI as an opportunity for humanity, rather than a threat. The swing to the majority, however, was represented by men, who were more optimistic than the women interviewed.[9] Other research in the UK suggests that views are influenced by education levels.

Onward, a UK-based think tank, found that most people surveyed with qualifications below graduate level were negative about the

8 A. Smith and M. Anderson, *Automation in Everyday Life*, PEW Research Center, 4 October 2017, retrieved on 3 September 2020 from <https://www.pewresearch.org/internet/2017/10/04/automation-in-everyday-life/>.

9 O. Buston, R. Hart and C. Elliston, 'An Intelligent Future? Maximising the Opportunities and Minimising the Risks of Artificial Intelligence in the UK', *Future Advocacy*, 2016, retrieved on 11 September 2020 from <https://futureadvocacy.com/wp-content/uploads/2018/04/Anintelligentfuture-3.pdf>.

impact of innovation on jobs and felt that the government should protect jobs at the expense of innovation.[10] Graduates and postgraduates, on the other hand, expressed support for innovation over protecting jobs, no doubt a reflection of how secure they felt about their own future work. In another survey for the same report 64% of people polled believed that computers or robots within fifty years of the report's date would do much of the work done by humans, with a majority of those surveyed thinking that people would find it hard to find employment then.

Clearly, there's public concern around the world about the impact of AI and robots on jobs, but what's the likely reality? Automation in the manufacturing sector, led by the automotive industry, has been around for many years. Today motor cars and electronics are the two largest areas of manufacturing where automation is used in the assembly of products. In this sector as a whole robots displace on average 1.6 workers after the first year of operation. Since 2000 around 1.7 million jobs have been displaced globally by industrial robots, with the majority of losses being in the USA, the EU, South Korea and China. At the end of 2016 China alone accounted for some 550,000 of the jobs lost in manufacturing.[11]

But what of the future? *Oxford Economics* estimates that some 20 million jobs will be lost by the end of 2030 due to the growth in manufacturing.[12] A global study, conducted by McKinsey Global Institute, puts the number of jobs affected by automation, not just in manufacturing, at between 75 million and 375 million by 2030, around 3–14% of the global workforce.[13]

These scenarios are based on an analysis of what jobs could be automated by known technology; although, as Brynjolfsson has commented, many jobs carried out by skilled workers may be

10 W. Tanner, G. Miscampbell and J. Blagde, 'Human Capital', *Onward*, 3 July 2019, pp. 31–33, retrieved on 16 July 2019 from <https://www.ukonward.com/wp-content/uploads/2019/07/ONWJ7193-Human-Capital-report-190626-WEB.pdf>.

11 Lambert and Cone, 'How Robots Change the World', p. 21.

12 Ibid.

13 J. Manyika, S. Lund, M. Chui, J. Bughin, J. Woetzel, P. Batra, R. Ko and S. Sanghvi, *Jobs Lost, Jobs Gained: Workforce Transitions in a Time of Automation*, p. 64. McKinsey Global Institute, December 2017, pp. vi, 2, 11, 77.

preserved, with automation improving productivity.[14] In their analysis, Manyika et al. show that while new jobs will be created as automation progresses, typically they will require both technical and soft skills, with the soft skills being required for the service and care industries.

In the *Oxford Economics* study the value created by robots in terms of efficiency, increased GDP and profit will offset the impact on employment, referred to as the 'robotics dividend'.[15] This, it's argued, will create more jobs, as demand and spending increase due to falling prices, increased income and higher taxes.

Looking at automation generally, rather than robotics on its own, the McKinsey study also predicts growth in employment, with up to 250 million new jobs being created by 2030 from new and additional work required to service demand for products and services. The McKinsey models show that rising incomes, followed by ageing healthcare, will by a significant margin contribute the most to creating new jobs. These jobs are widespread, with some manual and low-skilled work in construction, catering and hospitality but many requiring higher-educational qualifications and skills.[16]

This isn't a happy outcome for those who may lose their jobs and will find it hard or impossible to be reskilled. Many in low-skill jobs will not possess the soft skills required in the service industry.[17] In times past workers migrated from agriculture to manufacturing and those displaced from manufacturing have had to find work in the service sector. While it's true that the service sector has grown, this growth masks the fact that many who are having to transition will not have the ability to be reskilled for the jobs created.

Most studies agree that the real challenge will be in reskilling the workforce and helping people to transition from one job to another.

14 Erik Brynjolfsson, Tom Mitchell and Daniel Rock, 'What Can Machines Learn, and What Does It Mean for Occupations and the Economy?', *AEA Papers and Proceedings* 108 (2018), pp. 43–47.

15 Lambert and Cone, 'How Robots Change the World', pp. 35–37.

16 Manyika et al., p. 64.

17 The term 'soft skills' is used to describe a combination of interpersonal attributes, such as communication, social and relationship skills – sometimes also called people skills.

Despite this reality, most Organisation for Economic Co-operation and Development (OECD) countries have had a declining spend on training since 2000. Even with education being provided for most up to pre-degree or pre-vocational training level, will those left without work be able to retrain or improve their education to a level needed by these new jobs?

A sobering thought from an analysis of historic economic trends is provided by Manyika et al.: 'Although economies adjust to technological shocks, the transition period is measured in decades, not years, and the rising prosperity may not be shared by all.'[18]

Although it's difficult to predict the future, the rapid uptake of AI and somewhat slower deployment of advanced robotics will influence the less well-educated and poorer members of society, increasing the economic divide and tensions in society. Do we really want to see this trend develop for the sake of greater convenience, becoming more efficient and having more 'stuff'?

The UK government in its Modern Transport Bill states that its aim is to 'put the U.K. at the forefront of autonomous and driverless vehicle ownership and use'.[19]

We might ask the question 'Why?' The answer is surely that this is in some way important for the future of the UK's economy and prestige, especially given the competition around the world among governments to be seen to be at the forefront of the AI revolution. It betrays a lack of insight into the potential human cost of this revolution and the idea that to oppose technological progress is to be a Luddite all over again. The tensions are clear: unabated technological progress driven by profit, providing wealth for some but an uncertain future for others, with the prospect of comparative poverty and an accompanying loss of dignity. Today it really is different from times past, because, as we've seen, the issues go beyond the future of our jobs. Yet the way out for some is to pay people not to work.

18 Manyika et al., *Jobs Lost, Jobs Gained*, p. 48.

19 Cabinet Office, *Queen's Speech 2016* (18 May 2016), retrieved on 12 September 2020 from <https://www.gov.uk/government/speeches/queens-speech-2016>.

Free money

Suggestions for dealing with the threat to jobs include the idea of the state providing a guaranteed minimum income (GMI) or universal basic income (UBI). The idea of the GMI goes back at least to the eighteenth century and is seen as a system of social justice to deal with poverty. Many developed countries adopt some version of this for social welfare, such as providing a basic income during unemployment.

The UBI, as the name suggests, is a more universal basic income that all citizens would receive to compensate for lack of work or reduced working hours. At its heart it is simply a means of redistributing wealth, created in the case of AI by the companies that profit from it. Governments would levy high tax rates on these corporations in order to fund the UBI or GMI.

In 1976 Alaska established the Permanent Fund into which at least 25% of revenues generated from Alaska's mineral deposits, primarily oil, are paid each year and then invested into a variety of assets worldwide such as stocks and property. The aim of the fund is to benefit current and, in particular, future generations of Alaskans when the state's non-renewable resources, such as oil, run out. The fund was valued at over $65 billion in 2018 and an earnings reserve account is used to pay each citizen an annual dividend. The fund could be seen as an example of a type of UBI, but paid for in this case out of the revenues from natural resources.

Experiments have been proposed by proponents of UBI, such as Sam Altman, President of Y Combinator, a Silicon Valley business startup accelerator, to study the impact on people's lives of a small guaranteed income of $1,000 per month over three to five years. The pilot project was delayed by Institutional Review Boards and the need to ensure any recipients' social benefits would not be lost.

Shortly after the announcement of the trial in 2016, Elizabeth Rhodes, the research director for Y Combinator's UBI project, told online publication *Quartz*:

> If technology eliminates jobs or jobs continue to become less secure, an increasing number of people will be unable to make

> ends meet with earnings from employment. Basic income is one way to ensure that people are able to meet their basic needs. We're not sure how it would work or if it's the best solution, which is why we want to conduct this study.[20]

Finland, Canada, India and the Netherlands have already experimented with the idea of UBI with small numbers of recipients. While some of the experiments on UBI, such as those in Finland and Canada, have been stopped, they're in no way conclusive in terms of the potential success or failure of a mass roll out of UBI, assuming enough taxes could be raised.

The very idea of using UBI to alleviate the challenges to work that AI and intelligent robotics present raises significant questions. What will we do with the free time, and will recipients end up at the bottom of the economic pile, while the technology companies and their employees get rich? There are those who suggest that we'll move towards becoming a leisure society, freed from labour by the advances that we've made in technology.

Critics of UBI suggest that it's promoted by technology entrepreneurs out of self-interest, to deflect serious concerns about the impact of AI and robotics on employment:

> The trouble comes when UBI is used as a way of merely making techno-capitalism more tolerable for people, when it is administered like a painkiller that numbs the pain and masks the symptoms of economic injustice without addressing the root causes of exploitation and inequality.[21]

Without discussing further the motives behind UBI or its practicality, there's a more fundamental issue that we'll now turn to: whether we want a society in which work is replaced by leisure.

Some may think that this is a wonderful opportunity to pursue sports or other hobbies, or even to spend more time with people.

20 Cited in J. Sadowski, 'Why Silicon Valley Is Embracing Universal Basic Income', *The Guardian*, 22 June 2016, retrieved on 28 April 2020 from <https://www.theguardian.com/technology/2016/jun/22/silicon-valley-universal-basic-income-y-combinator>.

21 Ibid.

Surely, after all I've said about the threats to community and true relationships, that must be a good thing. How does this prospect relate to God's making Adam and Eve cultivate the garden, before the fall, which we saw in chapter 4? Let's explore this theme a little further as we seek to respond to the challenges to work that AI is posing.

Created to work

The early part of the book of Genesis lays a foundation for our thinking about work. From the opening lines of the text we see that our creator is a God who works in bringing his creation into being, and that he's satisfied with this work. In the early narrative about creation God commanded things into being: 'And God said, "Let there be light", and there was light. And God saw that the light was good' (Gen. 1:3–4).

When it comes to creating man, God is more intimately involved, using the 'dust' that he brought into being, as the expanded narrative in Genesis 2 shows: 'the LORD God formed the man of dust from the ground and breathed into his nostrils the breath of life, and the man became a living creature' (Gen. 2:7).

In the verses following we read of God's planting a garden and setting man within it to cultivate it:

> And the LORD God planted a garden in Eden, in the east, and there he put the man whom he had formed. And out of the ground the LORD God made to spring up every tree that is pleasant to the sight and good for food.
> (Gen. 2:8)

> The LORD God took the man and put him in the garden of Eden to work it and keep it.
> (Gen. 2:15)

All this occurred before the fall, so from this, coupled with the functional aspect of the *Imago Dei*, we can deduce that God intended humans to work in his creation. Not only that, but God also provided a helper for Adam, signalling that just as he's a relational God within the Trinity and with humans, so humans should be in relationship with others. A consequence of this is that men and women, even after the fall, share the workplace with their fellows. The fall, however, brings about a change to working conditions, as God curses the ground because of Adam's sin and tells him:

> in pain you shall eat of it all the days of your life;
> thorns and thistles it shall bring forth for you;
> and you shall eat the plants of the field.
> By the sweat of your face
> you shall eat bread,
> till you return to the ground,
> for out of it you were taken;
> for you are dust,
> and to dust you shall return.
> (Gen. 3:17–19)

Adam and Eve are then sent outside the garden of Eden, 'to work the ground from which [Adam] was taken' (Gen. 3:23). Although there are a number of aspects to why we work and what it's for, one basic reason is given in God's response to Adam cited above: we work to eat! This theme continues through the New Testament, with the apostle Paul's commanding the Thessalonian Christians, 'If anyone is not willing to work, let him not eat' (2 Thess. 3:10).

In his exposition of Exodus, Luther, in an amusing riposte, illustrates the importance of work in order to provide for our material needs:

> God does not want us to have success come without work . . . he does not want me to sit at home, to loaf, to commit matters to God, and to wait till a fried chicken flies into my mouth. That would be tempting God.[22]

22 Martin Luther, *Exposition on Exodus*, chapter 13:8, quoted in L. Ryken, *Work and Leisure, in Christian Perspective* (Eugene, Ore.: Wipf & Stock Publishers, 2002), p. 93.

There are other reasons that God 'calls' or requires us to work, including meeting the needs of others and serving the good of a wider society, as the prophet Jeremiah encouraged the Jewish exiles to do in Babylon:

> Build houses and live in them; plant gardens and eat their produce. Take wives and have sons and daughters; take wives for your sons, and give your daughters in marriage, that they may bear sons and daughters; multiply there, and do not decrease. But seek the welfare of the city where I have sent you into exile, and pray to the Lord on its behalf, for in its welfare you will find your welfare.
> (Jer. 29:5–7)

Various instructions in the book of Proverbs also underline the importance of work for the future of family and generosity to the poor:

> A good man leaves an inheritance to his children's children.
> (Prov. 13:22)

> The wisest of women builds her house . . .
> blessed is he who is generous to the poor.
> (Prov. 14:1, 21)

These sentiments are echoed in the New Testament:

> But if anyone does not provide for his relatives, and especially for members of his household, he has denied the faith and is worse than an unbeliever.
> (1 Tim. 5:8)

> And let our people learn to devote themselves to good works, so as to help cases of urgent need, and not be unfruitful.
> (Titus 3:14)

We see that not only has God created us to work, but work is an intrinsic part of what it means to be made in his image. Through work we display something of the nature of God, not only as a worker but also as someone who is creative in work. We image God in the way in which our work is carried out, providing for others and thus displaying love through work. If economists are correct about the future of work in an AI-driven economy, the dignity found in work may be lost by many. Some may argue that less work would give us more leisure time that could be spent in relationships, evangelism and caring for people. How do we square this circle?

Leisure is a cycle

Set alongside the fact that we're made to work is the equally important need to rest, shown by God himself, when he rested from his labours on the seventh day. God tells his people that they should also rest on the Sabbath, keeping it holy:

> Thus the heavens and the earth were finished, and all the host of them. And on the seventh day God finished his work that he had done, and he rested on the seventh day from all his work that he had done. So God blessed the seventh day and made it holy, because on it God rested from all his work that he had done in creation.
> (Gen. 2:1–3)

We may ask why God rested. It was certainly not because he was tired in the way that we become tired after a hard day's work. Rather, God has finished his work in creation and rests from that work, leaving humans to continue the creative work of subduing and stewarding what he has made. That God rested also sets an example for us to follow, as he commanded his people in the fourth of the Ten Commandments:

> Remember the Sabbath day, to keep it holy. Six days you shall labour, and do all your work, but the seventh day is a Sabbath to the LORD your God. On it you shall not do any work, you, or your son, or your daughter, your male servant, or your female

> servant, or your livestock, or the sojourner who is within your gates. For in six days the LORD made heaven and earth, the sea, and all that is in them, and rested on the seventh day. Therefore the LORD blessed the Sabbath day and made it holy.
> (Exod. 20:8–11)

God has established a cycle of work and rest that reminds us that he's at the centre of life and that our identity is in him. Life isn't all about survival, even in poor countries, or about job satisfaction and climbing the corporate ladder, in developed economies. Nor is it simply about productivity, efficiency and economics.

This concept of rest isn't nullified by Jesus' teaching his disciples, 'The Sabbath was made for man, not man for the sabbath' (Mark 2:7), when they were criticized by the Pharisees for plucking heads of grain on the Sabbath. The Pharisees said that this was against the law, meaning no work should be done on the Sabbath. But Jesus' teaching here is about the avoidance of legalism. In other words, keeping the law for the law's sake, rather than understanding and acting on the principles behind the law.

For Christians this means we're not to be legalistic about working on Sundays, but should recognize that there is a purpose in this cycle of work and rest. The purpose isn't just physical rest from our labours, important though that is, but is also to keep the day holy. That is, to remember God's creating work, to worship and give glory to him.

It's clear that the natural order for humanity is a cycle of work and rest, with work being part of what it means to be created in his image. In particular, as we saw in our earlier consideration of what it means to be created in his image, humanity has a role in stewarding natural resources. For the Christian this takes on a more significant responsibility in seeking to restore that which is broken through the fall, making God's creation more as he intended until the new kingdom is finally and fully ushered in. We live now between the reality that 'the kingdom of God has come' (Luke 11:20), of which Jesus spoke, but also that this kingdom is 'now but not yet'. The kingdom will be fully realized when Jesus returns and we will see 'a new heaven and a new earth'.

We can see that from the beginning of creation we've always tried to improve the way in which we work, making it less burdensome. In just six generations after Adam we read in Genesis 4:20 of Jabal's being 'the father of those who live in tents and have livestock'. By this time tents had been designed and perfected with the materials then at hand. Livestock were being reared and entertainment was available through music, fostered by the invention of musical instruments, Jubal being 'the father of all those who play the lyre and pipe'.

We read of Tubal-cain's being a 'forger of all instruments of bronze and iron', suggesting that by this time the use of agricultural and other instruments had become well established. Human inventiveness, particularly in the area of technology to improve food production and to reduce the labour required, has continued apace. As we saw in chapter 3, the twenty-first century isn't the first time that humanity has faced a widespread disruption to work, the Industrial Revolution being a case in point. Although new jobs were created, with the middle classes emerging as a result of new requirements for accountants, people to service machinery and later healthcare and education, the current disruption of work may result in fewer new jobs.

This should be of concern to Christians because, as those created in God's image, our world view ascribes a dignity to work itself. The functional view of *Imago Dei*, being vicegerents or stewards over his creation, also makes it difficult to see how we should rely entirely on technology to perform this on our behalf while we rest, rather than work alongside this technology.

What does it do to the dignity of a man used to stacking shelves for a living to be told that he's redundant because a robot can do the job just as well, twenty-four hours a day, and it doesn't need rest? Do we want to consume 'art' created by an AI computer, whether music, stories or pictures, rather than foster true human creativity?

What about replacing specialist skills in medical image interpretation or diagnosis with AI? Regardless of how good such technology may be or whether it may even be better than people doing the same job, the cry is often heard when such scenarios are posited 'What are we here for?'

I believe that these cries go to the heart of what it means to be human. Technology is in danger of replacing work and creativity, except for the elite few entrepreneurs, businesspeople and their staff who invent, develop, manage, market and service it. Is this the sort of society that pleases God and reflects his image?

As Christians, finding resonance within a wider society, we can be those who voice the importance and dignity of human work. We can be those who strive to find a balance between technology and humanity, erring on the side of caution and preserving rather than eliminating work, with the as yet unknown and perhaps unintended consequences to civilization of such an elimination.

Kai-foo Lee in his book *AI Superpowers* suggests job areas that AI won't be able to replace and that these 'safe areas' may create more jobs in the service sector, where human contact, creativity and specialism are vital. More physical jobs would include dog trainers, physical therapists and hair stylists. In Lee's vision specialist jobs such as those of social worker, CEO and psychiatrist may also be safe from AI or robots.[23]

Church leaders must also be careful to avoid deepening the sacred–secular divide by suggesting that universal basic income and job replacement by AI and robots would free Christians for 'full-time ministry'! For many Christians 'full-time' Christian ministry or service means to serve as a pastor, missionary or evangelist. The constant use of the term 'full-time' in the description tends to create the idea in our minds that this is more valuable and more important than any other work or service that we do for God – full time!

Although the Reformation, and especially Luther's writing, did much to correct the popular view in the Middle Ages that being a priest was a higher calling than being a tailor, the church has unwittingly slipped back into that frame of thinking:

> the works of monks and priests, however holy and arduous they may be, do not differ one whit in the sight of God from the

23 K. Lee, *AI Superpowers: China, Silicon Valley and the New World Order* (New York: Houghton Mifflin Harcourt, 2018), p. 155.

works of the rustic labourer in the field or the woman going about her household tasks . . . all works are measured before God by faith alone.[24]

The apostle Paul, when writing to the Christian church at Colossae, reminds them that whatever they do they should do it for Christ, not just for worldly masters: 'Whatever you do, work heartily, as for the Lord and not for men' (Col. 3:23).

Luther also saw the importance of doing whatever we do to God's glory and because God has bidden us to do it. In typical Lutheran style he puts it like this:

> If he is a Christian tailor, he will say: I make these clothes because God has bidden me do so, so that I can earn a living, so that I can help and serve my neighbour. When a Christian does not serve the other, God is not present; that is not Christian living.[25]

This manner of working can be seen as the 'good works' that Jesus speaks of to his disciples when he says, 'In the same way, let your light shine before others, so that they may see your good works and give glory to your Father who is in heaven' (Matt. 5:16). Dan Cathy, President of American food outlet Chick-fil-A, puts it pithily when allegedly referring to his drive-in outlets, 'In the same way, let your light shine before others, so that they may see your clean parking lots and give glory to your Father who is in heaven.'[26]

Our work means something to God, and the way in which we perform it should glorify him. It's difficult to see how a robot or an AI application gives glory to God in the same way!

---

24 E. H. Herrmann, *The Babylonian Captivity of the Church 1520: The Annotated Luther Study Edition* (Minneapolis: Fortress Press, 2016), p. 81.

25 Martin Luther, 'Sermon in the Castle Church at Weimar' (25 October 1522, Saturday after the Eighteenth Sunday after Trinity), in *D. Martin Luthers Werke: Kritische Gesamtausgabe*, 60 vols (Weimar: Hermann Böhlaus Nachfolger, 1883–1980), 10/3:382 (my trans.), quoted in F. J. Gaiser, 'What Luther *Didn't* Say About Vocation', *Word & World*, col. 25 (4) (autumn 2005), p. 361.

26 Retrieved on 11 September 2020 from <https://real.life/women/god-centered-goals-for-the-new-year>.

Work is a fundamental part of a Christian theology, and because of the implications of the advance and widespread uptake of AI technology work is an important part of a Christian attitude and response to the AI scenario. Of particular concern should be the fact that those with the least skills may be the first to be replaced by automation, leaving them without the dignity of work.

These may be the very ones who would find it more difficult to be reskilled, even if opportunities were offered. More skilled individuals may find their skills being copied and surpassed by AI applications, leading not only to a deskilling and tarnishing of the image of God in us, as we saw in chapter 5, but also even pushing them to part-time work. Efficiency is once more in the driving seat, this time threatening the dignity in work and God's natural order. Leisure, as we saw, is also an important part of the natural order, but needs to be held in balance with work, the dignity work provides and the outworking of one aspect of being made in God's image.

There are those who suggest that increased leisure might not be a bad thing as it could provide more time for relationship building. I might be cynical, but I wonder whether people might not just spend more time in virtual relationships through social media or become addicted to the upcoming, totally immersive, virtual and augmented reality experience. It's to that topic that we now turn as we conclude our exploration of the impact of AI and robotics on humanity.

10
A mirror world or reality?

Launched in July 2016 Pokémon GO, a mobile phone augmented reality game, was downloaded over 100 million times in just one month. It has now been played by hundreds of millions of people in 153 countries. Players download a free application on to their smartphone and the challenge is to find a Pokémon character on a game map that uses OpenStreetMap and data from Google Maps, by physically moving around with the phone, whether in the countryside or a shopping mall.

When a Pokémon pops up, players can choose to see it overlaid on to the real world, seen through the smartphone's camera. Using the smartphone gyroscope, these characters move as the player moves around. The game includes Poke Stops, places on the map where wild or rare Pokémon may appear, and Gym locations where battles can be fought. Collaboration with the Starbucks chain allowed Poke Stops and Gyms to be added at thousands of their locations.

When a wild Pokémon is encountered the idea is to catch it by throwing a Poke ball at it by flicking it from the bottom of the screen. Of course, there are only so many free balls. How else would the publisher make money from a free application? Niantic has grossed over $2 billion since the game was launched in 2016, the most successful game ever.

People have become so engrossed when playing the game that a couple of men fell off a cliff in California and others have caused road accidents by trying to catch a Pokémon on a busy road. In August 2016, shortly after launch, a driver in Japan, distracted by playing the game, killed one woman and injured another, the first reported death.

In their report 'Death by Pokémon GO' researchers at Purdue University found a significant increase in road accidents in Tippecanoe County, Indiana, USA, following the introduction of Pokémon GO. Their projections suggested that it cost the county \$5.2 to \$25.5 million over the 148 days following the game's introduction.[1] Niantic now publish some safety guidelines to follow when playing the game, such as not playing while driving or riding a bike.

Although interest in the game has waned, what these accidents illustrate is just how addictive games can be, and especially when based on augmented reality.

Augmenting reality with a virtual world has become the goal of many companies around the world as they seek to overlay real places with virtual representations. The idea is they should feel real, not just a sequence of 2D images stitched together, as we see in Google's Street View. The aim is more like what Google Earth gives as a suggestion: the ability to fly around buildings or over a terrain, as if we were really there.

These are 'mirror worlds', a term coined by Yale Professor David Gelernter in his 1991 book of the same title.[2] They have depth and texture, giving us a sense of 'place'. Unlike virtual reality, which is observed through special glasses that block out the real world around us, augmented reality users see through glasses that enable them to see the real world at the same time.

Imagine a navigation system that overlays direction signs or describes objects or scenes as you pass them. The development of these virtual worlds will enable us to experience situations or parts of the world that we've never travelled to in ways that will feel just as if we were there. Creating a virtual scene of a fire, as an example, could allow firefighters to practise emergency procedures without the risk of being hurt.

---

1 M. Faccio and J. J. McConnell, 'Death by Pokémon GO: The Economic and Human Cost of Using Apps While Driving', *Social Science Research Network* (2 February 2018), retrieved on 19 November 2019 from <https://ssrn.com/abstract=3073723>.

2 D. Gelernter, *Mirror Worlds: Or the Day Software Puts the Universe in a Shoebox . . . How It Will Happen and What It Will Mean* (New York: Oxford University Press, 1991).

Microsoft's HoloLens will map the room or space where a user is wearing the glasses and then allow them to use their hands to manoeuvre computer menus and choose applications in a similar way to making gestures on a touch screen, rather like many sci-fi films have projected for some time! Microsoft's vision is the office of the future, where one can create as many virtual screens as one wants.

Imagine repairing a jet engine with an overlay of the engine in 3D that could point out where to look for problems, or being able to see what a piece of furniture looks like in one's home. Sally Huang, Head of Visual Technologies at home improvement company Houzz, says of their AR smartphone application, 'When shoppers try such a service at home, they are 11 times more likely to buy.'[3]

As we found with other AI applications, such as digital assistants, VR and AR applications divide between professional and consumer use, and the same trends to get consumers hooked are observed. Big Tech wants to capture the consumer world, where users can be sucked into immersive experiences, whether in gaming or shopping, to increase sales.

While applications may look tame today, no major technology breakthroughs are required to extend the breadth and depth of the technology to the point that our world is digitized and constantly updated by a myriad of sensors.

Who will own this data and how will it be protected? As things stand, probably Big Tech, with the consequence that once more privacy will be compromised. Already images of people's streets and houses are publicly available through Street Maps, whether we like it or not. Apple CEO Tim Cooke stated in a corporate earnings report in late 2017, 'Augmented reality is going to change everything, I think it's profound, and I think Apple is in a really unique position to lead in this area.'[4]

This virtual world is the foundation for applications such as self-drive vehicles that need a map of the world to navigate by using

---

3 K. Kelly, 'AR Will Spark the Next Big Tech Platform – Call it Mirrorworld', *Wired*, 12 February 2019, retrieved on 28 April 2020 from <https://www.wired.com/story/mirrorworld-ar-next-big-tech-platform>.

4 Cited in ibid.

sensors to update this virtual map with live data. The interconnectedness of such systems will of course create a real-time updated virtual world.

While at first sight such technologies may appear benign and helpful, as we saw in chapter 3 technology isn't neutral and, unfortunately for some, it can become addictive. Especially so in the case of computer games.

Losing reality

Virtual and augmented reality in entertainment have the potential to be highly immersive experiences, sucking users in to the point where they lose track of time and reality. Andrew Wilson, CEO of Electronic Arts, believes that 'One of the core reasons why we engage with games is for social interaction,'[5] yet his vision for the future seems contradictory, substituting a virtual world of social interaction for the real world. He expresses it in this way:

> Maslow's hierarchy of needs: once you get past air, food, water, shelter, you get to sense of belonging, which is really about socially interacting. You get to self-esteem, which is really about overcoming challenges, and you get to self-actualization, which is really about creating in a living world. Games are going to give you all of those things. I think what we start to see is less about [what the game is] – is it a shooter, is it a sports game, is it open world or closed world, is it a linear story or a forked story, is it multiplayer – and more about this one, existing world where we all play a part.[6]

Perhaps that's why he believes that 'Your life will be a video game'.[7] Can we really substitute virtual communities for real physical

5 C. Plante, 'Your Life Will Be a Video Game: Andrew Wilson, CEO, Electronic Arts', *Verge*, 16 November 2016, retrieved 19 November 2019 from <https://www.theverge.com/a/verge-2021/ea-ceo-andrew-wilson-interview-virtual-video-games>.

6 Ibid.

7 Ibid.

communities where we sit next to each other, walk and talk, do things together or share a meal?

Entertainment is a touchy area for Christians, but gaming and VR are a slippery slope. While our children might enjoy playing a virtual game of football, wouldn't it be better for them to kick a real ball with friends and get some exercise? The very real danger of course is that an immersive experience that's fun at first rapidly becomes addictive without real discipline. We end up losing a huge amount of time and real relationships.

The challenge of virtual worlds, even those that are AR, is whether we'll in the end be able to distinguish between what's real and what's fake. The more our simulated world looks like the real world, the more we'll treat it and its simulated people in the same way we would the real world. We explored the evidence for this when we looked at the impact of personified digital assistants on human interaction in chapter 6. The same dangers that we observed when using Alexa, 'digital humans', toy or humanoid robots are present in virtual or augmented reality experiences. In addition, virtual worlds lay us open to manipulation, especially when used in applications such as shopping.

Having a chance to try something at home, without the inconvenience of visiting a shop only to find the item isn't in stock, sounds attractive. It would certainly be more convenient, and for busy people may free up time for other activities. But as we know, predictive algorithms in online shopping try to make us buy more stuff, and the virtual reality or augmented reality experience in the comfort of our home is likely only to increase that temptation.

Perhaps the effects seem slight at first glance, but how will we know when we're being manipulated through an all-too-realistic virtual reality? Will convenience and the seduction of VR result in our losing interaction with real people in a real shop?

Apart from the existing evidence of addiction to technology such as computer games and social media, it will be hard to predict what the future will hold as AR technology develops. As *Wired*'s founding executive editor Kevin Kelly puts it:

> The emergence of the mirror world will affect us all at a deeply personal level. We know there will be severe physiological and psychological effects of dwelling in dual worlds; we've already learned that from our experience living in cyberspace and virtual realities. But we don't know what these effects will be, much less how to prepare for them or avoid them. We don't even know the exact cognitive mechanism that makes the illusion of AR work in the first place.
>
> We reflexively recoil at the spectre of such big data. We can imagine so many ways it might hurt us. The great paradox is that the only way to understand how AR works is to build AR and test ourselves in it.[8]

And that's exactly what's happening now: the technology is being built and tested, but not in a controlled way. It's as if we were simply just wanting to find out what it did to us without thinking about it first.

A slippery slope

What we can predict – if we allow such technology to diminish those aspects unique to our humanity – is the likely impact on what it means to be human: our ability to love, to form real rather than fake relationships, to have freedom to choose rather than be seduced. As Kelly has stated, we don't really know how such applications will influence our minds as we transit between worlds or meld them together.

The danger is that these virtual worlds become our 'real' world, the place where we find ultimate meaning. Virtual worlds displace the real world that God made and we can end up exalting this virtual world we've created, enthroning it, and by so doing dethroning God.

When we substitute a virtual world for the real world and become immersed in it, not only does it dethrone God, but it diminishes our

8 Kelly, 'AR Will Spark'.

humanity, ultimately affecting our health, as other addictions have demonstrated. It becomes nothing less than idolatry. Indeed, all the other application areas of AI share the same danger of fostering idolatry, when we become dependent on them, extol them and credit them with a potency that belongs to God. The risk of idolatry in the ways in which we use AI technology is significant and we'll therefore need to dig a little deeper into these assertions.

When God wrote down the Ten Commandments on tablets of stone for Moses on Mount Sinai, the first command was that the chosen people should 'have no other gods before me' (Exod. 20:3). God spells out what this means and the consequences of their displacing him:

> You shall not make for yourself a carved image, or any likeness of anything that is in heaven above, or that is in the earth beneath, or that is in the water under the earth. You shall not bow down to them or serve them, for I the Lord your God am a jealous God, visiting the iniquity of the fathers on the children to the third and the fourth generation of those who hate me, but showing steadfast love to thousands of those who love me and keep my commandments.
> (Exod. 20:4–6)

From their earliest days the children of Israel oscillated between obedience to God and lapsing into idolatry, the worship of man-made entities. Isaiah, somewhat mockingly, accuses the Israelites of making useful implements out of iron and keeping warm by burning wood, yet out of the same material creating an idol or god to fall down to and worship! He accuses them further of 'praying' to it and saying, 'Deliver me, for you are my god!' (Isa. 44:17). Earlier in chapter 6 of Isaiah's prophecy, he laments that 'they bow down to the work of *their* hands, to what *their* own fingers have made' (Isa. 2:8; italics mine).

The psalmist in Psalm 115:4 also refers to idols of silver and gold as 'the work of man's hands'. Yet they're inanimate, having no mouth to speak or ears to hear, and the psalmist concludes that

> Those who make them become like them,
> so do all who trust in them.
> (Ps. 115:8)

G. K. Beale explores this theme in his book *We Become What We Worship*, where he traces the idolatry from the prophet's warnings back to the fall of Adam and then through into the New Testament. Beale argues from the prophet Isaiah's writing on idolatry that 'if we worship idols, we will become like the idols that we worship and that likeness will ruin us'.[9] A stark warning, but can we really conceive of AI technology becoming an idol? Surely that's a stretch too far. In order to answer that question, we need to understand what the Bible teaches about the nature of idolatry, beyond mere statues of wood and stone.

Today a developed Western culture may typically think that we're superior to ancient cultures because we no longer carve images in wood and stone or cast metal objects in silver or gold and make them our deities. At heart, however, idolatry is simply revering something else more than God, or putting our reliance in it. Alex Motyer defines it as 'whatever claims the loyalty that belongs to God alone'.[10]

When Adam and Eve were tempted to eat of the forbidden fruit, they displaced God's moral authority and took it upon themselves to make the rules. Of course, the devil seduced them by questioning God's moral authority when he said to Eve, 'Did God actually say . . . ?' (Gen. 3:1). Effectively, they, the created ones, chose to act as if they were gods, taking upon themselves the moral authority that was their creator's and putting themselves in control. Chris Wright, in his book *The Mission of God*, puts it this way:

> God accepts that humans have indeed breached the Creator-creature distinction. Not that humans have now become gods

9 G. K. Beale, *We Become What We Worship: A Biblical Theology of Idolatry* (Downers Grove: InterVarsity Press; Nottingham: Apollos, 2008), p. 46.

10 J. A. Motyer, 'Idolatry', in *The Illustrated Bible Dictionary*, ed. J. D. Douglas (Leicester: Inter-Varsity Press, 1980), vol. 2, p. 680.

> but that they have chosen to act as though they were, redefining and deciding for themselves what they were to regard as good and evil. Therein lies the root of all other forms of idolatry: we deify our own capacities and thereby make gods of ourselves and our choices and all their implications.[11]

Summarizing these observations, Wright suggests, 'The primal problem with idolatry is that it blurs the distinction between the Creator God and creation.'[12]

This is precisely what's happening when we think that we can create a machine in our image, even one that we think is cleverer than we are, a superintelligent artefact, a *Homo Deus*. We look to it to solve our problems, to save the world and give us freedom, and in so doing dethrone God. Not only that, but we effectively end up displacing humanity, which is made in God's image.

New idols

There are, however, I believe, more subtle and nuanced ways in which we could be in danger of creating idols out of AI. To understand this assertion, we need to think a little more about the nature of idols or gods.

Wright argues that there are different kinds of gods, and that we're 'in large measure responsible as human beings for the gods we create'.[13] Interestingly, the different effects of AI applications that we explored in previous chapters map on to some of the things Wright suggests we manufacture gods from – things that entice us, things that we trust and things that we need.[14]

We've already seen that AI applications can be designed to be seductive and enticing, making it easier to search, try things out in our home and buy them. Often this is achieved by the personification of AI, where we simulate human characteristics, such as the ability

11 C. J. H. Wright, *The Mission of God* (Nottingham: Inter-Varsity Press, 2006), p. 164.
12 Ibid., p. 187.
13 Ibid., p. 166.
14 Ibid., pp. 166–171.

to hold a conversation, watch a person, react to and display emotions or sense other aspects of our environment.

As we noticed in the prologue in Ellie's response to her mother, there are also dangers when we begin to regard these artefacts as 'oracles', trusting them to know more than we do, or even to be better than us. What about AI applications that we allow ourselves to rely on for medical image matching for diagnosis, or risk assessment in the judiciary? Sex robots become idols, designed to meet the real human needs that are part of how God has made us, and in so doing displace humanity.

Another potential for idolatry is where we assign moral agency to an AI computer or robot: we give it the ability to make moral choices without human intervention. We argue that it's creating a safer world and put our trust in it. In reality we're diminishing our humanity, the image of God in us, by transferring moral decision-making to an artefact that we've made in our 'image'. What also of our dependence on God and our acceptance that until Jesus comes our world will always be imperfect because of the consequences of sin? Of course, in general terms, whenever we trust or revere anything more than God, whether it be technology, money or our status, it becomes idolatry.

Hardly a day goes by without some headline extolling the virtues of AI in solving this or that problem, whether it be a new drug discovery, more efficient cities or a medical diagnosis that trumps human ability. During the Covid-19 pandemic governments and Big Tech have shown us how we can counter the virus's spread through the use of tracking and modelling data from our mobile phone's whereabouts. Some indeed wonder whether these applications could be the salvation of our world from future virus attacks.

Another tower

What's driving this enthusiasm and funding frenzy for AI? On one level, the protection and betterment of society seem to be good ends if we can save lives, prevent another pandemic or get to work more reliably. The danger is that beneath the desire to see society flourish is a darker desire: to become masters of our universe, or even achieve immortality. The long-term quest for general and superintelligence isn't only driving a mass of applications of AI now; it is also creating an expectation that this technology will be the saviour of humanity. Governments around the world are racing to get ahead of the game, in the belief that this technology is crucial to the future well-being of their citizens, as well as their economies.

The hype and expectations surrounding AI and its application is in danger of giving rise to a generation that thinks the technological progress of humanity is unstoppable, and one is reminded of a similar arrogance, millennia ago when humans tried to build a tower reaching to the heavens:

> Now the whole earth had one language and the same words. And as people migrated from the east, they found a plain in the land of Shinar and settled there. And they said to one another, 'Come, let us make bricks, and burn them thoroughly.' And they had brick for stone, and bitumen for mortar. Then they said, 'Come, let us build ourselves a city and a tower with its top in the heavens, and let us make a name for ourselves, lest we be dispersed over the face of the whole earth.'
> (Gen. 11:1–4)

God's response to this technological prowess and quest to make a name for themselves is clear:

> And the Lord came down to see the city and the tower, which the children of man had built. And the Lord said, 'Behold, they are one people, and they have all one language, and this is only the beginning of what they will do. And nothing that they propose to do will now be impossible for them. Come, let us go down and there confuse their language, so that they may not understand one another's speech.' So the Lord dispersed them from there over the face of all the earth, and they left off building the city. Therefore its name was called Babel, because there the Lord confused the language of all the earth. And

> from there the Lord dispersed them over the face of all the earth.
> (Gen. 11:5–9)

Likewise, King Nebuchadnezzar, the most powerful ruler of the vast Babylonian Empire, who reigned from 605 to 562 BC, in glorifying his 'majesty' allowed pride and arrogance to take over regarding his achievements. Not acknowledging his creator, 'the Most High', as the one who rules the world, led to his downfall:

> All this came upon King Nebuchadnezzar. At the end of twelve months he was walking on the roof of the royal palace of Babylon, and the king answered and said, 'Is not this great Babylon, which I have built by my mighty power as a royal residence and for the glory of my majesty?' While the words were still in the king's mouth, there fell a voice from heaven, 'O King Nebuchadnezzar, to you it is spoken: The kingdom has departed from you, and you shall be driven from among men . . . until you know that the Most High rules the kingdom of men and gives it to whom he will.'
> (Dan. 4:28–32)

You may ask: isn't AI just a progression of man's creativity, deriving from our being image bearers? Not when our creativity ends up dethroning God, by transferring our dependence on him to creation – to an artefact we've made out of our fallen imagination.

The prophets Jeremiah, Isaiah and Ezekiel all pronounced that Israel's reliance on the nations of Assyria and Egypt amounted to idolatry. This was because they were trusting in something other than God for their future:

> Have you not brought this upon yourself
> by forsaking the Lord your God,
> when he led you in the way?
> And now what do you gain by going to Egypt
> to drink the waters of the Nile?

Or what do you gain by going to Assyria
  to drink the waters of the Euphrates?
Your evil will chastise you,
  and your apostasy will reprove you.
Know and see that it is evil and bitter
  for you to forsake the LORD your God;
  the fear of me is not in you,
declares the Lord GOD of hosts.
(Jer. 2:17–19)

In the book of Revelation we also see that God views Rome's rule as being against God's rule, because they set themselves up as gods. Not only do nations and kings replace God when it comes to whom or what we trust in for the future, but humans too, from their earliest days on earth, have developed a dependence on technology. King Uzziah started his reign well in about 790 BC:

> he did what was right in the eyes of the LORD, according to all that his father Amaziah had done. He set himself to seek God in the days of Zechariah, who instructed him in the fear of God, and as long as he sought the LORD, God made him prosper.
> (2 Chr. 26:4–5)

During his long fifty-two-year reign he accomplished much under God's hand, creating cisterns to provide water for his herds and for irrigation, equipping his army with weapons and inventing new weapons as well as other forms of defence:

> Uzziah prepared for all the army shields, spears, helmets, coats of mail, bows, and stones for slinging. In Jerusalem he made engines, invented by skilful men, to be on the towers and the corners, to shoot arrows and great stones.
> (2 Chr. 26:14–15)

Yet towards the end of his reign, when he became strong, he became proud of his achievements and this led to his destruction. Perhaps he relied too much on his technology and achievements, thinking that what he had made would secure Israel's and his future. This story is a powerful reminder that while we may invent many useful items of technology or even discover new things, we must not rely on them nor become proud of our achievements.

Universities and corporations are becoming proud of what they have invented and the potential of these inventions for greater efficiency, convenience and better health. Some see themselves as agents of human flourishing and creating a better society. The widespread application of AI, however limited it may be, is creating false expectations and fostering a world view that believes technology is our saviour.

From a Christian world view we can see that this amounts to a form of idolatry, just as the apostle Paul warned Timothy of the dangers of relying on money. Jesus warned his hearers about reliance on possessions for their future, by telling a parable of a rich fool:

> And he said to them, 'Take care, and be on your guard against all covetousness, for one's life does not consist in the abundance of one's possessions.' And he told them a parable, saying, 'The land of a rich man produced plentifully, and he thought to himself, "What shall I do, for I have nowhere to store my crops?" And he said, "I will do this: I will tear down my barns and build larger ones, and there I will store all my grain and my goods. And I will say to my soul, 'Soul, you have ample goods laid up for many years; relax, eat, drink, be merry.'" But God said to him, "Fool! This night your soul is required of you, and the things you have prepared, whose will they be?" So is the one who lays up treasure for himself and is not rich towards God.' (Luke 12:15–21)

Although there's no prohibition on technology per se in the Bible, the message is clear: that we must not look to it or depend on it for our future. The fact that so many people are using personal assistants and that AI generally is being seen as empowering humanity, or that it may even be a 'saviour' of humanity, is creating a society that relies on technology rather than on God.

Key, then, to whether AI becomes an idol is both what we do with these artefacts and our motivation in creating them in the first place. Do we serve them, do we rely on them rather than on God for our well-being and do we glory in what we've made? Are they designed to manipulate, to appeal to our vulnerabilities, to mimic what's unique about our humanity with a view to replacing us? Ultimately, the question for us is how seriously these applications dishonour God by tarnishing his image in us and diminishing our image-bearing responsibility.

A pale reflection

When God commanded his people not to make images of him or anything in his creation with a view to worshipping or revering them, he did so because he has already made an image of himself and that's us! As we saw in chapter 4, he has also made us his representatives in the world.

Isaiah mocked Israel because they made images that couldn't talk or hear, smell or taste, and that were not able to move. Current AI technology and intelligent robotics can take on human attributes, and in one sense we could argue that they can speak and hear, see and move.

It's my belief that creating an artefact in our image runs the danger of diminishing our own personhood, especially when we delegate our image bearing to something that we've made. It's because God has made *us*, not our creations, to be his image bearers and to carry the responsibility for stewarding his creation.

When we create a machine to be like us, and allow that machine to have the responsibility of a human, we deflect and diminish his image in us. Isaiah speaks of how an Israelite carpenter takes a block of wood and 'shapes it with planes and marks it with a compass. He shapes it into the figure of a man, with the beauty of a man, to dwell in a house' (Isa. 44:13). Idolatry distorts the image of God in us and in so doing deprive God of the glory due to him.

Part of our worship of God is being his image bearers and in so doing bringing glory to him. We reflect God's kingship by being his vicegerents, a role unique to humankind. We must take care not to diminish or tarnish that special role by creating simulations of humanness to act on our behalf. We cannot simply see AI as a proxy for humanity in this regard by arguing that since God made me and I made the technology, ergo it has the same status as me. An artefact has no soul, no moral freedom to choose to love, serve and worship God.

Many have argued that technology is neutral and what we do with it determines whether it becomes an idol. I argued in chapter 3 that technology isn't in fact neutral: it's designed by people with an aim and with design attributes that reflect their desires, world view and, indeed, fallen nature. These aims may be, as so often occurs in AI applications, to exploit our vulnerabilities, to get us addicted to the technology, which influences our thinking and behaviour – sometimes without our realizing it.

Chatbots that behave like humans are a classic case in point and we've already noticed that we tend to respond to them as if they were human. Their impact on children has also been noted in terms of a child's tendency to command and be rude, so much so that Amazon changed Alexa's response to praise politeness.

The danger for Christians is being unwittingly sucked into certain types of technology, including AI. We find out after the fact that we're being shaped by it, that our behaviour is being modified by it in destructive ways that relate to what it means to be human.

We're made for relationship with God and with our fellows, and it's a dangerous path we tread when we turn to simulated humans for relationship – when we allow our view of ourselves and what we've made to be shaped by this simulated humanness.

Commenting on the threat of robotics and AI to jobs and the vested interest that Silicon Valley has in the technology, Jeremy O'Grady in an editorial in *The Week* writes, 'It isn't that artificial intelligence is becoming more human. It's that human intelligence is becoming more artificial, more conformist, more rule-bound.'[15]

15 J. O'Grady, 'Editorial', *The Week*, 6 July 2019, p. 5.

Isaiah told the children of Israel that they would become like the idols that they worshipped. We too will become like the AI that we worship if we delegate aspects of our personhood to it, because we'll blunt our cognitive and emotional acuity as we increasingly rely on AI to make decisions.

AI isn't human: it's an illusion of humanness and human intelligence. It in fact lacks any real intelligence, and if we revere these artefacts, however clever they may appear, we also will become non-intelligent. Regarding the ungodliness and unrighteousness of humans, the apostle Paul says, 'Claiming to be wise, they became fools, and exchanged the glory of the immortal God for images resembling mortal man and birds and animals and creeping things' (Rom. 1:22b–23).

Although it's not my belief that we can replicate the human brain, many are convinced that it's simply a matter of time, requiring only cleverer algorithms than we currently have along with enough computing power. With this prospect in view, such technology opens up the possibility for many of achieving immortality, either by AI solving ageing or by allowing an upload of our brain into a computer to live for ever – provided the power isn't turned off!

In the process of becoming immortal and solving the problem of ageing, humans thus become the deity, the *Homo Deus* Harari speaks of. There's nothing new in this quest, and the problem of humankind from the beginning was that Adam wanted moral autonomy, desiring to become like God rather than serve him. We know where that got us, and seeking to develop AI that will release us from the bonds of death will not only lead to disaster. It is a fool's errand. Death will not be overcome by humans, because Jesus has already done that, and he alone provides a remedy whereby we may live for ever with our creator. Yet many who do not believe in God are caught up in the allure of immortality that they see AI and other technologies offering; even beyond that the possibility of becoming gods, outshining humanity as we know it.

In search of immortality

Yuval Harari predicts that having substantially solved the problems of war, disease and food, 'humankind is likely to aim for immortality, bliss and divinity' in the twenty-first century, although he admits that this may not be achieved; it will be the collective aspiration, rather than the desire, of every individual.[16]

The transhumanist movement has emerged over a few decades and is united around the philosophy that humankind can be enhanced, in lifespan and intelligence, beyond our human limitations through science and technology. Its founder, philosopher and futurist Max More, defined the philosophy in an essay in 1990:

> Transhumanism is a class of philosophies of life that seek the continuation and acceleration of the evolution of intelligent life beyond its currently human form and human limitations by means of science and technology, guided by life-promoting principles and values.[17]

This philosophy is an extension of humanism and posits that eventually humans could become totally transformed, so-called posthuman entities with superior intellect and lifespan to humans. Posthumans could become resistant to diseases and ageing, perhaps through advances in nanotechnology and genetic engineering, or they could exist as uploaded and synthetic entities. Other visions of this posthuman future include enhancement of humans by a combination of technologies such as AI. Transhumanism is the intermediate state between our current limitations and the posthuman dream.

This vision sounds remarkably like the vision of the builders of the tower of Babel, a vision where we reign supreme over our environment and future, even our decaying bodies. It's to be expected

16 Y. N. Harari, *Homo Deus: A Brief History of Tomorrow* (London: Harvill Secker, 2016), p. 64.
17 M. More, *Transhumanism: Towards a Futurist Philosophy*, 1990, retrieved on 3 September 2020 from <https://web.archive.org/web/20051029125153/http://www.maxmore.com/transhum.htm>.

of a people who have dispensed with their creator and dismissed the very notion of a God who rules over them and their world.

These are powerful forces, and, as Harari points out, although not everyone will agree to or even desire this future, it could become a generally accepted aspiration of society. As Christians we must therefore be aware of these forces and be clear about our own future, as well as God's view of those who seek immortality without him.

To see technology in all its forms, whether AI or genetic engineering, as a saviour is to deify technology and displace God from his rightful place in our thinking. This is no less than modern idolatry and we must beware that we're not unwittingly sucked into it.

God's mission is to restore creation to its full original purpose of bringing all glory to himself and thereby to enable all creation to enjoy the fullness of blessings that he desires for it. God battles against all forms of idolatry and calls us to join him in that conflict.

The true *Homo Deus*

The quest to become immortal, and in so doing to become a god, a *Homo Deus*, fails to recognize that there's a man who already is *Homo Deus*, our Lord Jesus Christ. Jesus was in the bosom of the Father from all eternity (John 1:18), perfect and with all power and authority upholding the world by his power and might. Yet this perfect Son of God became flesh and dwelt among us. Though he was perfect and truly God, he did not count this equality with God (John 5:18) something to be grasped but became obedient to death, even death on a cross for our sake.[18]

Jesus' death was precisely to deal with our limitations, brought about by sin, not a slow process of supposed evolution that has stopped short of perfection. Death is a result of the fall, and our desire to become like God without obedience to him is no less than to want to become gods. Jesus deals with the problem of death once and for all time in his death as a punishment for our sin and rebellion against God. It's only by facing up to our sins, confessing them

18 See Phil. 2:6–8.

before God and accepting Jesus into our lives that we can be rescued from the penalty of death.

The true *Homo Deus* is the only way to immortality, but he requires that we die to self and pass through death into eternal life with him. These are well-known realities that we must cling to and proclaim to a lost world that seeks immortality through its own endeavours and the technology it creates.

11
Soul purpose

This book has focused almost exclusively on the potential threat that various AI applications pose to our personhood, but AI isn't an entirely negative force. There are many applications that have little or no impact on the image of God in us, nor our ability to reflect that image. These are applications that I call 'passive' and we may not even be aware of many of them, such as facial recognition to open one's smartphone or the algorithms in a phone camera that determine the correct exposure for a scene that one has chosen. Although even here one could argue that the easier it is to take a really good professional-looking photo on a smartphone, the less we'll need skilled photographers! For the time being, though, there's still a real art to creating the right composition. As an amateur photographer myself, I still prefer my single-lens reflex (SLR) camera over my iPhone for serious shoots, although as the old adage goes, the best camera is the one you have with you!

Whether we like it or not, AI in its various guises is forming us and shaping who we are, especially the more humanlike it becomes. Applications such as digital assistants become habit forming without our really being aware of it. This technology, along with digital technology generally, is alienating us from some part of our lives, our real humanness that's the image or nature of God in us. It's shaping our sentiments and what we love, almost without our being aware, because everyone else is caught up in it. It has become a mediator between us and others, between us and our world – it has become a digital priesthood.

A digital priesthood

The more humanlike and convenient AI technology becomes, the more it erases the distinction between online and offline, while at the same time creating an illusion of more control of our lives and our digital world. Yet the evidence is that this technology is already beginning to control us. Children, for example, find it hard to take off the 'lens' through which they see and interact with the world. Digital technology, and increasingly AI, *is* their world. This technology has become another priesthood, a mediator through which we interact with other people and through which we understand our world. Many have become reliant on this technology and are uncomfortable when it's taken away, finding themselves insecure and struggling emotionally to deal with people face to face.

Much of this is driven by an asymmetry of power between Big Tech and consumers. Big Tech is owning more and more of our souls as we lose freedom, privacy, authentic relationships and moral accountability. Even the state is embracing this technology, whether it be to improve our security, control the spread of viruses or simply to reduce labour costs and increase efficiency.

All of this is happening in the context of an assumption that technology and AI are progress, and that progress is good and will result in human flourishing. The evidence, however, is stacking up that humanity is far from flourishing, although ironically a few are flourishing financially, at the expense of their products – the human users whose data they sell.

It's time for us to realize that digital technology, and AI in particular, is having a profound effect on our souls and is leading us into captivity to the artefacts that we've made. The multitude of ethical guidelines being produced around the world, as we'll see in the next chapter, aren't going to provide the answer. Rather, we need to reclaim our souls by setting boundaries for our engagement with AI and imitate Christ's behaviour. It's he alone who can empower as the one who has set us free from bondage to sin and our 'old selves'. How, then, might we be able to set these boundaries for our engagement with AI?

Reclaiming our soul

Our starting point is to recognize and celebrate the distinctiveness of what it means to be human, what it really means to be made with something of the divine nature. Although the image of God in us is affected by our sin and desire for moral autonomy, Christ has freed us from slavery to sin.

This freedom was gained at a great price, the death of our Lord Jesus Christ who bore the punishment for our sin and rebellion against God. This Jesus, the true *Homo Deus*, rose again from the dead, gaining victory over death and Hades and judgement. It's this Jesus who calls us to take up our cross and follow him, this Jesus who prayed to his Father that he would keep us from evil and that he would sanctify us in the truth (John 17:15–19).

Jesus also proclaimed that we're not of this world, just as he isn't, even though we're to remain in the world until he comes or calls us home. The apostle Paul goes on to work out the practical implications of these truths and, when writing to the Corinthian Christians, urges them to be 'imitators of me, as I am of Christ' (1 Cor. 11:1). Paul similarly exhorts the Christians in the church at Ephesus, 'Therefore be imitators of God, as beloved children. And walk in love, as Christ loved us and gave himself up for us, a fragrant offering and sacrifice to God' (Eph. 5:1–2).

We see a symmetry between Paul's two exhortations, to imitate Christ and to imitate God, because both share the same nature: 'He is the image of the invisible God, the firstborn of all creation' (Col. 1:15).

To imitate Christ is to imitate God, which is no less, as 'new creations', than to display the Father and Son's image and nature.

What does it mean to imitate God and to imitate Christ? We've already seen that part of the nature of God is love, and Jesus, who is one with God, shares the same nature with him, demonstrating his love for us by giving himself up for us.

Imitating God and Christ is a command for us to image the Godhead, to allow the nature of God, in whose image we're made, to shine forth. This means that we must be careful to avoid those things that diminish or tarnish that image, those attributes of God such as true love, the expression of which is made possible by the freedom regained through the cross. John amplifies these thoughts in his first letter:

> Whoever says 'I know him' but does not keep his commandments is a liar, and the truth is not in him, but whoever keeps his word, in him truly the love of God is perfected. By this we may know that we are in him: whoever says he abides in him ought to walk in the same way in which he walked.
> (1 John 2:4–6)

We're to keep his word and his commandments in order that the love of God in us may be perfected. The way that we do this is by walking, behaving, like Jesus. This isn't a passive walk but one that involves warfare as we battle the forces of darkness that would drag us down and diminish the image of God in us. As followers of Christ we're exhorted to put off the old self and put on the 'new self, which is being renewed in knowledge after the image of its creator':

> Put to death therefore what is earthly in you: sexual immorality, impurity, passion, evil desire, and covetousness, which is idolatry. On account of these the wrath of God is coming. In these you too once walked, when you were living in them. But now you must put them all away: anger, wrath, malice, slander, and obscene talk from your mouth. Do not lie to one another, seeing that you have put off the old self with its practices and have put on the new self, which is being renewed in knowledge after the image of its creator.
>
> Put on then, as God's chosen ones, holy and beloved, compassionate hearts, kindness, humility, meekness, and patience, bearing with one another and, if one has a complaint against another, forgiving each other; as the Lord has forgiven you, so you also must forgive. And above all these put on love, which binds everything together in perfect harmony.
> (Col. 3:1–10, 12–13)

Paul points out that our new self, the new me, is being renewed in line with the image of our creator. This is an ongoing process, not a once-for-all experience, so we must pay attention to the impact that the world around us, including technology and AI, has on the renewal of our self. Be in no doubt, we're engaged in a spiritual battle against the forces of darkness. The devil will seek to subvert the process of our sanctification, our becoming more like Christ. We need therefore to be careful when engaging with technologies such as digital assistants, designed to appeal to our vulnerabilities, lest they subvert that process by causing us to become more like the old self, rather than being renewed in the image of Christ.

The image of God in us, although tarnished by sin, is being renewed to be a better reflection of the original image. If we allow ourselves to become immersed in technology that diminishes the true image of God in us, we're not cooperating with the Holy Spirit, who is the one who helps us to put off the old self and to put on the new:

> But when one turns to the Lord, the veil is removed. Now the Lord is the Spirit, and where the Spirit of the Lord is, there is freedom. And we all, with unveiled face, beholding the glory of the Lord, are being transformed into the same image from one degree of glory to another. For this comes from the Lord who is the Spirit.
> (2 Cor. 3:16–18)

In order to 'keep in step with the Spirit' we have to be thoughtful about how we use technology, especially seductive technology that on the surface seems harmless, simply convenient, the 'way things are done'! These are huge challenges for us as Christians, who are so easily squeezed into the patterns of behaviour of the world around us. Paul appeals to the Roman Christians when he writes to them not to allow themselves to be conformed to the world, but to change the way they think:

> I appeal to you therefore, brothers, by the mercies of God, to present your bodies as a living sacrifice, holy and acceptable

> to God, which is your spiritual worship. Do not be conformed to this world, but be transformed by the renewal of your mind, that by testing you may discern what is the will of God, what is good and acceptable and perfect.
> (Rom. 12:1–2)

In his book on the Sermon on the Mount, John Stott makes this observation: 'Probably the greatest tragedy of the church throughout its long and checkered history has been its constant tendency to conform to the prevailing culture instead of developing a Christian counter-culture.'[1]

The transformation that Paul talks about is an ongoing process, because he's saying that, as we change our thinking, we're able to see from his Word how God wants us to behave. This leads to an ability to discern the right way to act and behave, the right things to do and the things to avoid. It's no less than the reclaiming of our soul, the transformation of my old self into the new, which is in the likeness of Jesus.

The Bible is clear that we need to be careful to nurture our soul, otherwise, in this fast-paced digital age, such technology will gradually destroy our soul. This means understanding the effects of technology such as AI on our soul and being thoughtful about how we engage with it. Let's look at some practical steps we might take to assess the impact of AI applications on ourselves and what we can do to avoid their destructive influence.

Some practical steps

When Paul told the Roman Christians that they needed to change their thinking so as not to conform to the world around them, he was implying that they needed to understand both how the world thinks and how God thinks, so that they could see the difference and act accordingly. In his classic book *The Contemporary Christian* John Stott calls this idea 'double listening':

1 J. Stott, *The Message of the Sermon on the Mount*, revised edition (London: Inter-Varsity Press, 2020), p. 45.

> We are called to the difficult and even painful task of 'double listening'. That is, we are to listen carefully (although of course with differing degrees of respect) both to the ancient Word and to the modern world, in order to relate the one to the other with a combination of fidelity and sensitivity.[2]

The first step in our 'double listening', in order to reclaim our soul, is to be aware of what digital technology and AI are doing to us, how they're shaping us, what aspects of our humanity we're in danger of diminishing. Another aspect of 'double listening' is to understand what God is saying to us through his Word and what response that demands of us when living with this technology. That has been the purpose of most of this book and Table 1 opposite summarizes the key ways in which our humanness is potentially influenced by AI. I devoted a chapter to each of these key areas and these are referenced in Table 1.

Having understood the impact of AI on humanity, our next step is to look at how we use these AI applications and to think through the risks in using them. How are we personally being affected and what can we or should we do about it? Some applications of AI, in my view, cross a boundary and we should not allow them, because they're so clearly in contradiction to what it means to be human. For many other applications there's a spectrum of risk, dependent in part on how much we engage with them and how we control them. We'll consider this further in the next section.

Most Christians are concerned not to be labelled a Luddite in their attitude to technology and we must not forget that there are many applications of AI that are passive: they have little or no impact on our humanness. We can therefore rightly embrace them as useful artefacts and aides to our work, our life and living. But the purpose of this book has been to explore the risks of AI to being human, so our focus is on these, rather than an exploration of the good things that we can do with AI. We begin with applications that cross those boundaries I mentioned earlier.

---

2 J. Stott, *The Contemporary Christian: An Urgent Plea for Double Listening* (Leicester: Inter-Varsity Press, 1992), p. 13.

Table 1 Summary of the key effects on the image of God that we bear against the different types of AI applications that we considered in chapters 5–10

Taxonomy of AI applications	*How our soul is influenced*
AI replaces cognitive skills (Chapter 5)	**Loss of our minds** When AI learns and carries out skilled tasks that humans perform, replacing these tasks with automation leads to a loss of reasoning power, decision-making acuity and creativity.
AI simulates humanness and/or creates bonding (Chapter 6)	**Loss of relationships** Over-engagement with digital assistants, robot toys, healthcare robots and the use of sex robots fosters personification of artefacts and the development of non-human relationships that alters our ability to maintain or form true relationships with other humans. Our children's emotional and social growth is stunted and their ability to empathize is diminished along with the emotional maturity needed in normal human relationships and social interactions. Personification of artefacts leads to feelings of ethical obligation and the desire to assign rights to personified artefacts, amounting to idolatry.
AI is used for surveillance of citizens, and personal data is exploited by companies (Chapter 7)	**Loss of freedom to choose and privacy** This results from the state's surveillance of its citizens whether through facial recognition and other traits or the amassing of private data for running smart cities. Freedom and privacy are lost due to the even greater amassing and processing of personal data by Big Tech for profit without any real choice for consumers. The free product or service offering model is an abuse of power because consumers are seduced by Big Tech's offerings without informed consent to their data use, which in any event would be impractical.
AI is given moral autonomy (Chapter 8)	**Loss of moral responsibility** When we assign moral agency to a robot, such as a self-drive vehicle, to make moral decisions on our behalf we effectively delegate a responsibility that's uniquely human.
AI replaces manual and skilled work (Chapter 9)	**Loss of work** The dignity of work is taken away as jobs are partially or completely replaced by AI and robots, except where the work is hazardous.
AI is used to create a virtual reality on its own or to augment the real world (Chapter 10)	**Loss of reality** A loss of a sense of what's real through immersion in virtual and augmented reality, a loss of self-discipline, self-determination and control through addiction with a resulting loss of true community from isolation and virtual relationships.

One application of AI that crosses a boundary is fully autonomous self-drive vehicles where we would have to assign moral agency to the vehicle. Deployment of such vehicles is still a long way off, not only because of the technology and road infrastructure developments needed, but also because issues of liability have yet to be thrashed out. Many, even Christians, may at first thought find a ban difficult to justify, even though many are in favour of a ban on autonomous weapons.

I've suggested that when the image of God in us is diminished, it's offensive to God if we allow that to happen in us all the time we have a choice – we sin against God. We also diminish our ability to be image bearers and therefore to be true imitators and followers of Christ. Isn't stepping into an autonomous self-drive vehicle with either known or unknown moral behaviour, which we cannot control, a step too far? It amounts to giving up moral responsibility, a crucial part of our humanity that mirrors God's moral nature.

Another boundary for me is the surveillance of citizens by using facial recognition, gait analysis and any other personal attributes. Of course, there's an argument that says we might prevent terrorist acts or even catch a criminal with such technology.

The Covid-19 pandemic has resulted in a plethora of AI applications being developed to fight the disease and its spread. These range from the benign use of machine learning to help in drug and vaccine discovery and digital mapping of where the virus might spread, to more invasive uses, such as tracking and surveillance of citizens. Applications have been developed in Europe to allow people to be tracked from anonymous mobile data, ostensibly to see if they are obeying social distancing, and to identify possible 'hot spots'. In China drones have been used to patrol public places, and in Russia surveillance footage has been scanned to try to identify recent arrivals from China.

Following the use of a smartphone application in China to track people who had been in proximity to others who had tested positive, many governments and health service providers around the world developed their own applications for such tracking.

Apple and Google teamed up to provide an application programming interface (API) for their mobile operating systems to allow better solutions to be developed. While not involving AI, these applications have raised similar privacy concerns as other surveillance applications.

Although it could be argued that voluntary participation in a tracking system to mitigate health risks may be justifiable, the worry is about where such applications might lead, were they to become compulsory.

In the case of facial recognition and analysis of other personal attributes, is the cost to our freedom and privacy, part of what it means to bear God's image, worth it for the sake of a little more safety? Is it worth it when we consider the injustices that inevitably result from such surveillance? Principles such as prevention of harm and respect for human autonomy, espoused by the AI ethics committees, from a Christian perspective, mean allowing others the dignity of being in God's image, and having freedom to choose. These principles are too easily violated by the use of AI-enabled surveillance, whether it be to track terrorists or to scan one's face at a train station barrier to let one through to catch a train.

Ultimately, the only way to avoid these boundaries being crossed is through legislation, which requires significant public opinion in favour and a willingness of politicians and legislators to go down that track. As we saw in chapter 7, that has already happened in regard to facial recognition in some parts of the world and could potentially be taken up across the Western world, at least were there sufficient public concern.

Much has been made in the popular press of the problem of data bias in what are sometimes called 'risk assessment' applications, leading to a variety of issues, from incorrectly identified faces to injustice for blacks in the criminal justice system to gender bias in recruitment. AI systems require a lot of data to train them, but this data may not necessarily be completely representative of the real world. This leads to bias in the match probability that the system delivers when new data is presented. It's one thing to find your smartphone recognizes other people as you if you're Asian – you have a choice whether or not to use it. But it's quite another to be refused bail because you're black. As we saw in chapter 5, a black girl accused of petty theft who had a record of juvenile misdemeanours was rated a higher risk of reoffending than an older white man who was a more seasoned criminal.[3]

Another problem inherent in most AI algorithms is the lack of transparency in how a decision is reached. By their very nature neural networks use hidden, and usually multiple, network layers to determine match probabilities from input data, and the reason for that probability of match cannot be explained.

It seems to me that we should avoid building such systems, however convenient and efficient, for two reasons. First, they can result in injustice; and second, they remove human moral responsibility for actions taken. Yet some see such AI applications becoming better than humans, less open to bias, and therefore to be preferred. The Bible is clear that God hates injustice and holds only men and women responsible. To delegate this responsibility to an artefact is offensive to God because it diminishes his image in us, his moral nature. At the very least, when automated systems are used there should be a right of appeal to an independent human tribunal. This will be achieved only through legislation and regulation to oversee compliance, but it won't be easy, given the enthusiasm of politicians and the vested interests of business.

As many have observed in the consumer arena, and even in the business world, the free use of data in exchange for a service, whether search, social media or data storage, comes at a high price to humanity. This will change only with a disruption to the business model pioneered by Google and copied by many others. It's my belief that humanity would suffer much less coercion to conform if no company or organization were allowed to offer free services in exchange for our data, whether browsing history or where we travel and shop.

---

3 J. Angwin, J. Larson, S. Mattu and L. Kirchner, *Machine Bias: There's Software Used Across the Country to Predict Future Criminals. And It's Biased Against Blacks* (23 May 2016), retrieved on 29 August 2019 from <https://www.propublica.org/article/machine-bias-risk-assessments-in-criminal-sentencing>.

The complexity of the food chain in companies such as Google means that we would have to sign hundreds of contracts to provide properly informed consent to the use of such data. However, legislating that no services should be offered for free that are contingent on our data being available would, overnight, put the brakes on exploitation of our data.

Much less harm would occur to our humanity were we to pay for services, knowing that our data remains secure and private, whether we're searching, browsing sites, using social media or travelling using satnav. Once again, such changes are the province of state legislation and the regulators. The only glimmer of hope lies in the growing concerns in the USA where there are suggestions that Big Tech should be broken up, rather like what happened to the telephone company monopoly in the USA in the 1980s. However, this would not solve the problem were the business model to remain the same!

Although there are some applications of AI that may end up crossing a boundary of acceptability in terms of their impact on our unique humanness, there are others that require discernment in their use.

A spectrum of risk

In many applications of AI the impact on being human tends to be more of a spectrum of risk, rather than being outright harmful. Having understood how AI could diminish our image bearing, the best way to respond to the potential impact of an application on humans is to ask what authentic image bearing looks like and whether that's being diminished in me.

We could for example ask what authentic relationships look like and whether my, or my child's, relationships are being influenced by using, say, digital assistants or virtual reality. Table 2 (on p. 192) shows the nature of true relationships versus how digital assistants and other forms of humanlike artefacts tend to shape such relationships. A set of questions (columns three and four) helps us to evaluate how we might be influenced and some of the choices we have in response.

Table 2 Example of the difference between authentic relationships and the negative impact AI, used in digital assistants such as Alexa, could have on these through the way it forms us, alongside self-analysis and our choices

Characteristics of true image bearing in authentic relationships	*Influence of digital technology and personified AI*	*How am I being formed by AI and digital technology?*	*What are my choices?*
• Love • Commitment • Kindness • Preferring others over ourselves • Encouraging one another • Listening • Empathizing • True intimacy	• Abrupt communication • Inability to pay attention • Lack of focus • Diminished ability to reflect and think • Preferred because: – don't answer back – empathetic – easier to deal with – do what one commands • Gender stereotyping • Personification • Accept answers unquestioningly • Reliance on device	• How much time am I spending in a digital world vs the real one? • Which do I prefer? • Do I prefer to text? • Do I pay attention to others and listen? • Do I find it easy to empathize? • What are my expectations of others? • What am I prepared to give in relationships? • How do I view others, such as women? • Can I live without it?	• Give preference to face-to-face over virtual • Use text search and a neutral search engine instead of a digital assistant • Limit use • Ask whether it can be done another, more human, way • Avoid

Resolving tensions

What should we do when there are tensions between the use of an AI application, such as surveillance for security, and human freedom? Or self-drive vehicles that may save lives and human moral agency? Is it right to make trade-offs between two moral principles, and does the greater good always trump our conclusion? Might there be uses for AI that the majority are comfortable with but that could conflict with Christian ethics?

Our world view plays an important role in determining how we resolve these ethical dilemmas, and what we regard as non-negotiable values and principles. The drift towards naturalism in the West has caused people to dispense with God and the accountability that he requires and, as a result, an external moral compass has been lost.

While natural law, the idea that the moral law is written on all men's hearts, serves to sensitize people to what's right and wrong, they have no rationale for these feelings. As a consequence, abandoning God leaves society with a natural conclusion that decisions should be made for the greater good, so-called teleological ethics.[4]

Utilitarian ethics, which is a part of this philosophy, considers what's in the best interests of the majority. In creating rules for an autonomous vehicle, to determine what should be done when faced with a potentially fatal accident, the likelihood is that utilitarian ethics will lean towards the lesser of two evils. This may mean saving the most people or preferring to save a woman and child over an old person using a walking stick. Massachusetts Institute of Technology's Moral Machine experiment provides the public with an opportunity to decide what they would do when presented with a variety of scenarios that a machine might be required to act upon.

It's not too much of a stretch to imagine AI being trained from data collected in such experiments, in order to create a decision engine. Is this really where we want society to go – being driven in vehicles that act according to a majority vote?

World view has another important outcome when it comes to determining whether a robot should have rights. This may be to protect a robot from abuse or to provide it a legal status, such as a corporation has, potentially insulating the entity from its owner. A materialist view sees no distinction between a human and any other material 'substrate', such as silicon used in computer chips. This paves the way for granting the same rights to an 'intelligent' android robot, or machine, as a human on the basis of what's called 'ontogeny'[5] and 'substrate' non-discrimination.

Sophia, an android robot created by Hong Kong based Hanson Robotics, became the first robot to be granted citizenship at an AI business event in Saudi Arabia in 2017. This sparked a Twitter storm when people commented that the robot, which had no male guardian nor a head covering, had more rights than Saudi women.

---

4 From the Greek *telos*, meaning 'end' or 'purpose'.

5 Two beings can have the same function but differ in how they came into being, an example being in-vitro fertilization versus normal fertilization.

Most AI ethics guidelines fall shy of recommending rights to robots. Christians definitely ought to fight shy of giving rights to something that we've made, because humanity occupies a unique position in God's eyes. Adequate provision is made in property law, in many countries, to criminalize deliberate damage to things that we own, so why does an artefact need 'rights'?

When there appears to be ethical tensions in the deployment of an AI application or robot, how do we resolve these from a Christian perspective? Are there always clear biblical principles that we can use to determine the right answer? It's my belief that what's virtuous provides a clear guiding principle for resolving conflicts between ideals, such as protecting the public and preserving privacy.

Virtue over convenience

In his first letter Peter encourages Christians to supplement their faith with virtue, or moral excellence, along with several other qualities, such as self-control and love, in order to confirm their calling; that is, to demonstrate that they're true Christians:

> His divine power has granted to us all things that pertain to life and godliness, through the knowledge of him who called us to his own glory and excellence, by which he has granted to us his precious and very great promises, so that through them you may become partakers of the divine nature, having escaped from the corruption that is in the world because of sinful desire. For this very reason, make every effort to supplement your faith with virtue, and virtue with knowledge, and knowledge with self-control, and self-control with steadfastness, and steadfastness with godliness, and godliness with brotherly affection, and brotherly affection with love. For if these qualities are yours and are increasing, they keep you from being ineffective or unfruitful in the knowledge of our Lord Jesus Christ. For whoever lacks these qualities is so near-sighted that he is blind, having forgotten that he was cleansed from his former sins. Therefore, brothers, be all the more

> diligent to make your calling and election sure, for if you practise these qualities you will never fall. For in this way there will be richly provided for you an entrance into the eternal kingdom of our Lord and Saviour Jesus Christ.
> (2 Peter 1:3–12)

There's some overlap of these qualities and the fruit of the Spirit – love, joy, peace, patience, kindness, goodness, faithfulness, gentleness, self-control – that Paul enumerates in his letter to the Galatians (5:22–23). Together, we might regard them as an outworking of moral excellence, or putting it another way, the outworking of the image of God in us. These are some of the practical ways in which we put on the new self that we considered earlier.

When thinking about what to do when AI applications throw up moral dilemmas, virtue should inform our response. The idea that good societies are virtuous has a long history and, as I've already pointed out, has some traction today in various parts of the world. The four main virtues that have survived for more than the two millennia since Plato first proposed them are *prudence* (or wisdom), *justice*, *temperance* (or self-control) and *courage*. Christians have added to these faith, hope and love. In the Bible we have various lists that accord with the four cardinal virtues on which Plato suggested the character of a good city hinges.[6] Although framed slightly differently, the idea of preserving a virtuous society is highlighted by the Institute for Electrical and Electronic Engineers (IEEE) Standards Committee for Ethical Design in AI.

The virtue-based process I am advocating is illustrated in Figure 2 (on p. 196). It's a process that builds on our analysis of the impact of AI on personhood and then allows us to determine what to do. This provides a framework for resolving tensions between preserving aspects of human nature such as freedom, and other laudable goals such as protecting citizens.

We've seen that Christians are to grow in virtue and to put off the corresponding vices, so there should be no issue with our agreeing

6 Plato, *The Republic*, Book IV.

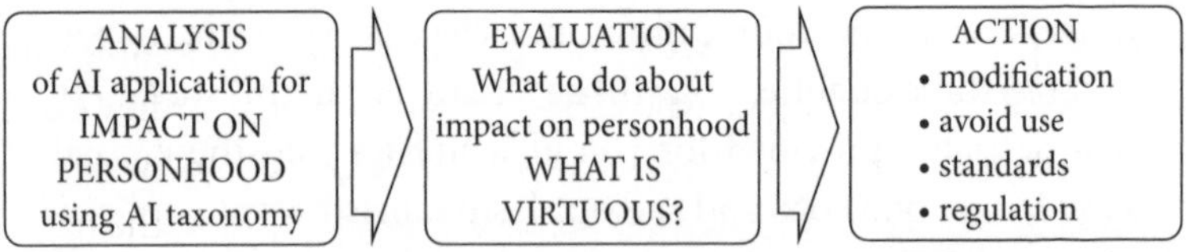

Figure 2 **A framework for evaluating the impact of AI applications on personhood and what to do about it**

to follow virtue in our evaluation of what to do with the effects of AI applications. It's also another facet of putting off the 'old self' and putting on the 'new self', created after Christ's image.

There are many who aren't Christians who may also subscribe to the idea that a virtuous society hinges, as Plato put it, on the four cardinal virtues. If we want to see a better society, or humanity flourishing, these cardinal virtues provide a powerful foundation and one that might resonate with some who aren't Christians. We might argue that this is something that we should encourage as part of what some see as the fulfilment of the creation mandate or, indeed, 'bringing in the kingdom'. This isn't of course to say that this alone will transform society – only embracing Christ will achieve that. Nonetheless, we have a responsibility to be virtuous ourselves and to encourage others to these virtues.

Let's look at some practical examples to see how this framework might be applied.

Predictive policing, using machine learning and other AI applications, is clearly something that police forces, and even government, might deem to be cost-effective policing. Such technology amplifies the resources available for tracking terrorists or criminals, and potentially provides safer societies, as no doubt the Chinese government would argue. Yet the downsides are wrongful arrests and loss of privacy and freedom of movement, as the leaders of the underground church in China have found. What's the virtuous way forward?

Justice and wisdom would suggest that the downsides outweigh the benefits, because it's better to have a free society that does not fear the state and the potential for wrongful arrest. They would look further to the example of other states and history and conclude that such technology could be used in overtly damaging ways to minority groups, such as Christians who are criminalized because they don't belong to a state-approved church. Millions of Uygars, likewise, are persecuted in China as a result of mass surveillance, all in the name of preventing terrorism. Is it wise to allow ourselves to slip down that path?

Courage would be required for us to follow the path of wisdom and justice and decide not to adopt such technology. These are decisions of the state, but citizens need to express their views and in some Western countries these are being solicited. Ultimately, the path of wisdom and justice may result in more, rather than fewer, terrorist threats or more criminal activity, but that's a balancing price to pay, and one that many societies may prefer over increasing state surveillance and control.

What about the dangers of personifying digital assistants or androids? How does virtue help in thinking about what should be done? Where simulated humanlike digital assistants engage us in dialogue, we're inclined to treat them in the way that we do humans. They begin to create empathy, leading to the feeling that they're owed ethical obligation and even rights, as people are. Some have proposed such rights to protect sex or child robots from abuse. What's the virtuous response to these dangers?

Using a sex robot is an extreme but sad example of where a human being resorts to a machine for selfish pleasure, pleasure that God intended inside a marriage relationship. Some have suggested that sex robots should be given rights to protect them from abuse. The wise way forward isn't to give any AI artefact rights, because in so doing we're conferring human status on it and demeaning humanity. Property law should protect the owner of the robot when it's damaged. Love would point to helping people with such addictions and problems, rather than giving them a robot substitute for the human relationship they crave.

Apart from sex robots, we find that the main driver for humanlike chatbots, avatars and robots is convenience and efficiency. Many businesses cannot, or do not, want to afford the level of human mediated customer service that we all would like, so many are rushing down the path of automation. On the surface it may seem ideal to have a customer service agent available 24/7, but what are the downsides of this convenience? If we lose out on real human-to-human interaction and the depth of knowledge that a human agent has, how do we as individuals and society at large benefit? We are in danger once more of efficiency and convenience luring us down the path of adopting such technology.

A wise and virtuous way forward would be to avoid being drawn more and more into a relationship with a machine, increasingly made by its designers to be more empathetic, more personable, to the point where we don't know what's real any more. Why is it necessary to create an artefact that behaves like a human? As a technologist and as one who was involved for many years in spoken language understanding, my answer would have been, 'Because we can, because it's fascinating and challenging!' Business competitiveness drives the deployment, offering more at lower cost to the business. Moderation suggests that we should put the brakes on such deployments and find ways to ensure that humans always know that they're interacting with a machine. Wisdom suggests that we should prefer human contact to a machine substitute and avoid the dangers I've outlined: of tarnishing the image of God in us.

A radical proposal is to ban the use of realistic avatars in customer services for businesses and government institutions. Do we really need to replace human contact with a simulation of a human that fools us into thinking it cares, when it has no soul or consciousness? Perhaps it would be wrong to ban using robots in care for children and the elderly, but their use requires very careful thought, particularly by the relatives. Raising these concerns should at least provoke such consideration, and maybe proponents of AI should stop trying to fool people into thinking that we've created human intelligence!

One of the key virtues that the Bible urges us to display is self-control, a virtue that avoids our becoming ensnared by the desires of the flesh, and that allows us to be discerning in how we use technology, and especially AI. Many, through a lack of self-control, have fallen into addiction, whether to social media, games or their Fitbit health monitor. The pace of implementation of AI and related technology will require us to be prepared and to be able to exercise self-control, and maybe even complete abstinence.

Many AI applications have significant consequences for both the individual and society in terms of the use of our private data, activities and location. While we may benefit in terms of efficiency and convenience and the state may savour the control it gains, do we really want to lose our freedom and privacy? Big Tech has a self-interested agenda, to make it as easy as possible to search, buy products and services and interact with a plethora of 'things', all of which provide data, the oxygen that sustains its business.

The virtues of justice and courage worked out would suggest that all of our data should by default be private. Courage would be required to legislate that no company or government should have access without consent. This would mean that all applications on smartphones, computers and electronic devices, including sensors, should default to a privacy setting, and businesses should not be allowed to access this data, at least not without informed consent.

Simply burying the consent in endless pages of 'terms and conditions' before one can use a search engine, or a purportedly free service, isn't sufficient. As I've already suggested, banning companies from offering free services in exchange for our data would blow apart their business model! Wouldn't it be prudent to pay for a search engine, or to subscribe to a social media platform, in exchange for total privacy and anonymity? Extending the argument to the state, we could also argue that governments should not have the right to collect images and data of their citizens and to monitor them without consent.

Thus far we've explored the impact that AI is having on our humanity against a backdrop of what it means to be human, to be made after God's image or in his likeness. We've seen that once understood, practical steps can be taken to enable us to use AI in a way that does not diminish the image of God in us, or subvert our ability to mirror that image. I've proposed virtue as a yardstick against which to determine what to do when there are ethical conflicts in the deployment of AI. Some applications should be no-go areas for Christians and we should, where we're able, influence legislators to ban their use.

In the final chapter I sum up these findings in a Christian manifesto and consider what's being done around the world to counter the negative effects of AI on society.

12
A Christian manifesto

In this book I've sought to outline the various ways in which certain current and near future applications of AI, including machine learning and intelligent robotics, have the potential to diminish our image bearing and thus our humanity. It has not been my purpose to spend time, other than in passing, outlining the benefits that can accrue from other applications of AI, but rather to focus on those areas that I see as challenges to our being faithful image bearers.

Notwithstanding several billions of dollars being poured into companies such as OpenAI and DeepMind to create general AI, the best that we'll achieve is likely to be a poor simulation of what it means to be truly human as I've defined it in chapter 4.

Yet, as we've seen, the challenges to humanity and civilization as a whole do not lie with the future capabilities of AI, but rather with the widespread and accelerating deployment of what can currently be achieved. We as individuals and as societies are already being shaped by this technology, without any serious public engagement or debate. Many of us have already been sucked in and are becoming dependent on this technology.

Christians are in a unique position to engage in such a debate and to provide moral guidance at a time when there's much concern and confusion. The pace of AI development and deployment is in the hands of a few extremely rich and powerful multinationals who, despite their ethical posturing, are no doubt more concerned to profit from this technological bonanza than to pause while civilization catches its breath.

I've presented a Christian anthropology as an essential foundation for beginning to think about how AI applications shape our humanity. This foundation is based on an understanding of what it means to be human and made in the image of God; that is, to share some of the essence of who God is. Humans are uniquely created by God to be in his likeness, a reflection of his character or attributes such as reason, love and creativity.

This foundation formed the basis for a more detailed analysis of how current AI applications are influencing different aspects of our humanness. These were summed up in the previous chapter in a taxonomy of AI application types, such as applications that replace cognitive skills, simulate humanness and take over moral autonomy.

We saw that an outworking of a Christian anthropology is that we're made to be God's representatives on earth, vicegerents or stewards of his creation. In this role we're God's icons, his image bearers. It's also clear from the Genesis account and elsewhere that part of being made to mirror God's nature means that we should be in a relationship with the Trinity and with other people. From this understanding emerged the principle that we should not allow our imaging responsibility to be tarnished or diminished by giving up part of what's uniquely human, such as decision-making or creativity, our moral agency or loving relationships.

God has also spelt out a moral code by which we should live in relationship to him and to others. This led to the principle of not making AI artefacts into an image of God through personification; that is, simulating sentience or delegated moral agency. We should not do this, because he has uniquely made humans as his image bearers. To do so amounts to idolatry.

Our views of humanity and concepts such as conscience and consciousness differ from those of naturalists, for whom the mind is just a computer that can eventually be replicated. However, to desire to create superintelligence is none other than a quest to replace God with our own god.

Furthermore, in our relationship with others God's moral law demands that we do not steal: we do not take something from another over which they have stewardship. This, we saw, has implications for freedom and data privacy, including data obtained from our activities and whereabouts by surveillance or through the internet of things.

The command not to bear false witness requires that we deal fairly with others. This means that we should not allow AI decision-making through data bias to influence others negatively. Not bearing false witness also requires that we don't deceive people by allowing them to believe that they're interacting with a human when it's a chatbot or another digital agent.

Work is a fundamental part of what God made us for, and therefore there's a dignity involved in performing it and having a job. We saw that God gave us a work and leisure cycle to follow and that we would not follow his calling by being permanently at leisure. Some have suggested that more leisure time would be a positive thing and have proposed that those without work could be paid a 'universal basic income'. This is a reversal of the natural order that the Bible teaches. These potential realities have huge implications for policymaking when it comes to replacing jobs, whether white or blue collar, with AI and robots.

We saw that although our soul has been corrupted by sin, the 'old self', Christians are urged to put on the 'new self' made after the likeness of Christ, who is himself the 'exact representation of God'. To live in obedience to God as true followers of Christ we're obliged to examine our daily walk with him and to determine whether AI applications, or any other human invention, help or hinder the life-long process of putting on the 'new self'.

Finally, I proposed the use of virtue as a criterion for determining what action we should take when faced with particular AI applications, and especially when resolving ethical tensions. It's my hope that this framework will stimulate others to think about how applications they're already using may be influencing them, or indeed whether to purchase or support certain uses of AI.

It's always helpful to have some practical steps we can take when faced with the challenges that technology such as AI presents to us, our children and even our grandchildren. An example of such steps was used in digital assistants such as Alexa in the table description (see Table 2 on p. 192). There I showed how they can distort the nature of true relationships and presented some key questions that we could ask ourselves to explore how they might be shaping us, and what we should do about it.

The more detailed analysis and conclusions from the previous chapters can be summed up in a set of propositions that could act as an overarching set of guidelines for the Christian community, a Christian manifesto for AI (see Panel 2).

Panel 2 A Christian manifesto for AI: managing the key impact areas on humanity

1 **Cognitive skills** – Where AI is used to replicate particular human skills in application areas that involve decision-making and that influence people's lives, humans should always make the final decision. The principles of justice and fairness must be upheld by allowing decisions to be challenged and requiring independent human review. Such applications must be audited and their performance reviewed on a regular basis.

2 **Human relationships** – Frequent use of artefacts that simulate human interaction has the potential to diminish our ability to relate to other human beings. People should always know they're interacting with such an artefact and it should not be assigned personhood or ethical rights. Such artefacts should be designed to signal that they're neither human nor a particular gender or persona; for example, by the nature of their voice or expression.

3 **Moral agency** – Humanity should not give up moral agency to an artefact such as an autonomous weapon or self-drive vehicle. AI intrinsically has no ethical or moral rights because it's an artefact made by a human. AI designers, owners and users should be held accountable through law and regulation for their use and actions.

4 **Work** – Automation of tasks that replace humans should be contemplated only where alternative work can be provided for those replaced. The dignity of work must be preserved and not replaced entirely by leisure.

5 **Reality** – We're created to inhabit and interact with the real world and for human relationships. We should be careful not to lose a sense of reality through exposure to virtual or augmented reality. Such systems should be designed to ensure users are aware of the difference between the virtual and the real and exposure may need to be time limited by the application.

6 **Privacy and freedom** – Every citizen's privacy should be respected together with freedom of movement and association. Data resulting from encounters with digital technology is private property and should not be collected and used by third parties, even when personal identifiers are removed, without informed consent. Given that this is mostly impractical, the use of digital products and services should not be conditional on such data being collected by the supplier nor any other third party. Digital surveillance of citizens is a breach of privacy and freedom and should be banned.

7 **Idolatry** – Certain deployments of AI will dehumanize civilization as we place more and more reliance on it and allow it to control our lives. This amounts to idolatry. Seeking to augment the human soul or to create superintelligence is to seek to become God and is also idolatry.

Propositions for humanity

These propositions provide a basis for how we ought to view and deploy AI applications and indeed whether there are some that we must avoid. The manifesto contains seven propositions for how we should regard AI, both now and in the future. These are based on the understanding that I elaborated earlier, of what AI can do to the image of God in us, our responsibilities as image bearers and stewards over God's creation. Six of these propositions map directly on to the six AI application areas of the AI taxonomy presented in chapter 11 and elaborated in chapters 5–10. The seventh proposition is a warning to us of the dangers of idolatry that I discussed in chapter 10, from over-reliance on and engagement with AI applications of different types. It also highlights the danger of pursuing superintelligence.

These propositions should serve to guide us in how we develop and deploy AI in order to ensure that humanity remains in control and that the image of God in us isn't diminished. This includes avoiding compromising our moral freedom, privacy, the dignity of work and doing what's right and just for others. The propositions do not limit the development nor the use of AI in areas where there's no impact on our personhood as I've defined it.

A sting in the tail

The detailed analysis of the preceding chapters and these propositions raise the question of what sort of society and civilization we want to live in. Do we want a society that's a pale reflection of true humanity through the dulling or loss of key human attributes; a fast-moving and efficient society, where everything is designed for our convenience, and where we can delegate responsibilities for our daily living to machines that decide what's best? Or do we want a virtuous society, one that embraces technology only so far as it assists in our mission and calling to be vicegerents and imagers of the only true God? These are pressing issues, not only for Christians but for civilization as a whole as the age of implementation of AI accelerates.

Experts, politicians and others from different faiths or no faith are recognizing that there are potential harms to individuals and society over the use of AI, in both the public and private arenas. It's widely recognized that this technology will reshape our civilization. While some are optimistic, seeing only the positive outcomes of technological progress, particularly efficiency and convenience, others are more cautious, seeing some of the negative consequences to humanity from the widespread deployment of AI that I've described.

There has been sufficient concern around the world, both from the public and private sector, to spawn numerous ethics committees and commissions, including government and standards bodies.

Ethics for all

Globally there are over eighty bodies advising on AI ethics and policy, with professional organizations such as the Institute for Electrical and Electronic Engineers seeking to develop a global set of design standards for 'Ethically Aligned Design' for AI systems. In the UK over fifteen public sector initiatives have been launched to advise on AI. The European Commission has a High Level Expert Group (HLEG) that has produced ethics guidelines for 'Trustworthy AI'.[1] This has subsequently resulted in a set of policy recommendations for the European Commission[2] and a White Paper outlining the likely political response to AI innovation and application.[3]

There's a good deal of overlap between the various reports and recommendations, with the importance of AI being for the common good standing out in most, alongside AI's not harming people or undermining their human rights. Human rights are often the basis on which the idea of human autonomy is founded and relates to individual freedoms as well as the right to have self-determination.

Clearly, surveillance raises issues as far as human autonomy is concerned, but often these high-level guidelines lack more specific recommendations. When it comes to preventing societal and individual harm from AI systems, although a laudable aim, these reports fail to spell out these harms adequately. More questions are raised by these reports than they answer. What does it mean for systems to be safe and secure, or technically robust, given the nature of AI algorithms?

The European Union High Level Expert Group's 'Ethics Guidelines' report suggests that

1 Independent High Level Expert Group on Artificial Intelligence, *Ethics Guidelines for Trustworthy AI*, European Commission, 8 April 2019.

2 Independent High Level Expert Group on Artificial Intelligence, *Policy and Investment Recommendations for Trustworthy AI*, European Commission, 26 June 2019.

3 European Commission, *White Paper on Artificial Intelligence – a European Approach to Excellence and Trust*, 19 February 2020, retrieved on 25 February 2020 from <https://ec.europa.eu/info/publications/white-paper-artificial-intelligence-european-approach-excellence-and-trust_en>.

> particular attention must also be paid to situations where AI systems can cause or exacerbate adverse effects due to asymmetries of power or information, such as between employers and employees, businesses and consumers or governments and citizens. Preventing harm also entails consideration of the natural environment and all living beings.[4]

As I've pointed out, there's clearly already an 'asymmetry of power' between Big Tech and consumers, and in some cases between the state and its citizens, as I've illustrated in regard to China's use of surveillance from facial recognition. Unfortunately, these reports stop short of recommendations where harms are already evident, and especially those that this book has sought to highlight.

Perhaps one exception to this is the Centre for European Policy Studies (CEPS) report *Artificial Intelligence: Ethics, Governance and Policy Challenges*. While containing many of the same terms as other ethics guidelines such as 'non-maleficence' (do no harm), protecting human integrity, security and privacy, the report is a little more specific about what these might mean for AI applications and, usefully, lists some 'problematic use cases and no go's'. One prohibited-use case is autonomous weapons, while 'problematic' examples are 'predictive policing, social credit scores, facial recognition and conversational bots'.[5]

What emerges from all these reports' concerns, however, is that there's likely to be a tension between the potential benefits from using AI systems and the impact on individuals and society. Perhaps this is why many reports fail to specify harms to society, or what should be done about them.

Jess Whittlestone and her colleagues suggest that while high-level principles in AI ethics are important, 'they may not be enough to ensure society can reap the benefits and mitigate the risks of new

4 Independent High Level Expert Group on Artificial Intelligence, *Ethics Guidelines for Trustworthy AI*, p. 12.

5 A. Renda, *Artificial Intelligence: Ethics, Governance and Policy Challenges* (Brussels: Centre for European Policy Studies, 2019), pp. 56–57.

technologies'.[6] The authors cite the example of bio ethics that similarly started with high-level principles, but in practice failed to deliver. They propose that the tensions between AI benefits and their negative influence should become the focus for AI ethical evaluations.

An example of tension cited by Whittlestone et al. surrounds a statement in the UK House of Lords AI Committee report that 'it is not acceptable to deploy any artificial intelligence system which could have a substantial impact on an individual's life, unless it can generate a full and satisfactory explanation for the decision that it will take'.[7] Whittlestone et al. suggest that this statement 'masks an important tension between using algorithms for social benefit ("beneficence") and ensuring those algorithms are fully intelligible to humans ("explicability")'.[8]

Many applications of AI are already in use today, such as assisting medical diagnosis and risk assessment, whose decisions, as I've already stated, cannot be explained due to the very nature of AI algorithms. Taking the House of Lords Committee recommendation at face value would exclude these applications from use. Who decides whether the benefits outweigh the effects on individuals or society, and what are the criteria?

Some of the applications in use, described in chapters 5–10, already conflict with a number of the guidelines and principles set out by various committees, such as not undermining human rights or harming people. This means that someone, either in government or in a corporation, has decided what's in the best interests of the individual or society. Someone has determined that a greater good is served by an application, even though an individual's liberty or even society at large may be harmed or human autonomy may be lost. It's expedient for private business and governments to have more AI applications because this means cost reductions and more profit.

6 J. Whittlestone, R. Nyrup, A. Alexandrova and S. Cave, *The Role and Limits of Principles in AI Ethics: Towards a Focus of Tensions*, Proceedings of the Association for the Advancement of Artificial Intelligence Conference, January 2019, pp. 195–200.
7 Ibid., p. 197.
8 Ibid., p. 196.

AI deployment is viewed to be better than existing practice, which is often dependent on humans. For the developers and suppliers of AI the driver is simply profit.

Decisions about what's best for society are often biased by the vested interests that sometimes conveniently coexist with the cultural norms in that society. China provides a case in point, where it would appear that there's an acceptance by the majority of surveillance, providing personal data and social scoring for the greater good. Surprisingly, given the controversy surrounding China's use of mass surveillance, the chairman of the Metropolitan Police Association, Ken Marsh, stated that it was 'spot on', and that the technology should be deployed across London on a twenty-four-hour basis. He went on to say that the use of facial recognition technology by Beijing was 'absolutely correct', while criticizing a report that questioned the legality of its use on British streets.[9]

While we may criticize countries such as China for the way in which they use AI technology in mass surveillance, we too have our own cultural biases when it comes to assessing whether AI is a good thing or not.

In the West most accept unquestioningly the benefits of free Google search, or the convenience of an Alexa personal assistant, without reflecting on the impact on our privacy or our humanness. Many have made the trade-off, if they're even aware of one, between efficiency and convenience, and privacy – along with the potential harm to what it means to be human.

The IEEE is one of the few groups that have sought consensus among different cultures and religious traditions on AI ethics, which challenges the goals of increased productivity at the expense of other measures of societal prosperity. Its committees have been drawn from several countries representing different ethical traditions, from Aristotelian to Confucian. In the introduction to their *Ethically Aligned Design* report the authors suggest that

9 M. Bridge, 'Use Facial Recognition Cameras Like China, Urges Police Leader', *The Times*, 9 July 2019, retrieved on 12 December 2019 from <https://www.thetimes.co.uk/article/use-facial-recognition-cameras-like-china-urges-police-leader-92f0rvc5s>.

> honoring holistic definitions of societal prosperity is essential versus pursuing one-dimensional goals of increased productivity or gross domestic product (GDP). Autonomous and intelligent systems should prioritize and have as their goal the explicit honoring of our inalienable fundamental rights and dignity as well as the increase of human flourishing and environmental sustainability.[10]

Such statements raise the question 'What do we mean exactly by human flourishing?' The report does, however, provide some elaboration by suggesting it to be 'the highest virtue for a society':

> Ultimately, our goal should be eudaimonia, a practice elucidated by Aristotle that defines human well-being, both at the individual and collective level, as the highest virtue for a society. Translated roughly as 'flourishing', the benefits of eudaimonia begin with conscious contemplation, where ethical considerations help us define how we wish to live.[11]

This means that there will be different interpretations of 'highest virtue' and 'human flourishing' among different people groups and societies, notwithstanding the latter term being a trendy and frequently used aspiration for society, even by Christians.

The tensions recognized between ethical principles arise from a conflict at a deeper level: between progress and virtue. This is brought out well in the IEEE statement cited previously, where they suggest that our goal should be a virtuous society, in an Aristotelian sense, not just one driven by increased productivity. Put another way, the tensions arising are between the desire for the progress that technology, and AI in particular, can bring about, versus creating a virtuous society.

---

10 The IEEE Global Initiative on the Ethics of Autonomous and Intelligent Systems, *Ethically Aligned Design: A Vision for Prioritizing Human Well-being with Autonomous and Intelligent Systems*, IEEE, 2019, retrieved on 1 August 2019 from <https://standards.ieee.org/content/ieee-standards/en/industry-connections/ec/autonomous-systems.html>.

11 Ibid., p. 4.

The danger of setting human flourishing as the goal for deploying AI applications is that we end up full circle and back to the Enlightenment view of flourishing. As we saw in chapter 3, since the Enlightenment of the late seventeenth and eighteenth centuries, progress has become one of the key tenets of Western thinking and aspiration. Philosophers in Europe began to see, to paraphrase Immanuel Kant, that we could think for ourselves and rely on our own intellectual abilities to determine what to believe and how to act. They believed that the greater good of society and liberty for the individual could be achieved through reason and scientific progress.

Philosophers such as John Locke espoused the thinking that life, liberty and property were important foundations of a good society. From this sort of thinking emerged the ideas of defining human rights, in order to protect life and liberty. Property laws in many countries emerged to defend the rights of citizens to own property and for others to respect these.

Scientific discovery leading up to the Enlightenment was often made by Christians who acknowledged God as the creator and so they held in tension the physical and metaphysical. The Enlightenment, however, led to a greater scepticism of the metaphysical and a reliance on human abilities to discover truth. This has led to naturalism, the idea that nature and the laws of nature are all there is. Darwin's theory of evolution strengthened this position, allowing scientists and others to dispense with God as the creator of the universe and humankind, because they now had another explanation for our origins.

The prevailing naturalist world view, with its emphasis on progress, has become a virtually unquestioned basis for human flourishing. Progress has now come to mean what's efficient and convenient, in an economic sense perhaps increasing gross domestic product, profit or global reach. As Christians we also have assimilated this thinking into our attitudes and behaviour as individuals, and collectively as the church. We assume by default that technology means progress and that it must be good and beneficial to us, the church and wider society. Efficiency and convenience have come to surpass other criteria for what's good.

Churches embrace the technology that allows multisite churches to develop and flourish, at least numerically, while worship becomes a multimedia sound-and-light show. We allow people to comment on the sermon via tweets from their smartphones, or to make a donation in a church service by hovering a credit card over a touch reader collection plate. Our own homes are full of gadgets in almost every room to make life more efficient, productive and fun. In these and many other ways we've become pragmatic in our thinking as individuals and as a church, adopting a mindset that as long as it works it must be all right.

While many outside the church are raising concerns over the impact of AI on humanity, Bible-believing Christians are uniquely placed to provide moral leadership and to become a community that truly reflects God's image as he intended. Of course, we need to take responsibility for our own use of AI, but church leaders also need to educate their members and think through how leadership is shown in this area, both personally and in the life of the church. Parents and youth leaders must engage with children and young people to begin a dialogue and create awareness.

Following Christ has never been an easy option, and in our hi-tech age sacrifices are involved, decisions must be made and things avoided if we're to be true disciples. This will be hard for many and especially young people, when digital technology and, increasingly, AI applications are all around and form the basis for how society operates. It will take courage to be different and to find alternatives for the convenience that the seductive technology all around us offers.

We need to create church communities that stand and work together, showing a different way to live. Encouragement comes when we know that we're not alone in battling the encroachment of technology. This is as true for children as it is for adults, yet so many feel the peer pressure to conform and don't see alternatives to the digital world that they inhabit. Working together as parents and families, we can pray for the courage to be different, to find alternative ways of doing things and to encourage our children to stand together as they also take up the challenge. We may be surprised to find others in our communities outside the church whose concerns resonate with ours, and who want to be part of doing things differently.

While there's a push towards creating 'trustworthy AI', even going as far as having product markings and standards approvals, I believe that this is dangerous because it doesn't address the core effects on humanity. It focuses on important but subsidiary issues such as data bias and transparency. In essence many AI applications are just opaque algorithms, trained on a vast amount of data. As we've seen, this data could be skewed, and how the probability of input data matching this database was reached cannot be known. We cannot think of AI in the same way that we might think about constructing a safe or 'trustworthy' bridge for traffic to cross, because in bridge design the engineering principles are well understood, verifiable and transparent.

The issue that we face as a civilization isn't whether AI is or can ever be made trustworthy, but how we can use it wisely, given its limitations and the way it shapes us.

Clearly, there are many areas in which AI and machine learning could be used without detrimental impact on human lives. Deep learning can improve the efficiency of heating systems in saving energy, which not only has a positive impact on a company's profitability but also helps to preserve natural resources.

On the other hand, similar deep-learning algorithms used to determine whether a first-time offender is likely to reoffend have a significant impact on the life of that individual. Humans alone should bear the responsibility for those decisions, however imperfect, because whereas a human can be challenged, an AI system cannot! We've seen that such systems could be skewed, even unintentionally. It's unlikely that we could ever be confident that an AI system was not skewed, because humans would have to make that judgement! Although humans are biased, the very nature of free societies is that human decisions can be challenged, even though that's a far from perfect process.

The narrative around AI often dwells on the idea that it will be fairer and better than us, even with these limitations, so let's stick with it and make it even better. At the end of the day, the issue isn't whether AI might be better at making decisions, whether about choosing a job candidate or determining parole. If we believe that God has uniquely created humans with moral freedom and responsibility, we must not cede these aspects of humanity to artefacts that we've made. To do so is to undermine the natural order, and is idolatry. Let us not look to technology to be our saviour, to deal with our sinful imperfections, but let us work towards improving our social structures and systems, and how we behave within them. That will create a more virtuous society and follow God's plan for humanity. It's to put humanity firmly in control of AI, rather than allowing it to control us.

These challenges are huge and in some areas will require the state to take action on our behalf if we're to ensure that we're masters over that which we've created.

There are many uses of AI where we have freedom to choose and to exercise self-control, either by moderation or abstinence, whether they be digital assistants such as Google Home, satnav systems, browsers or tools in our workplace. The challenge arises when we have no control or choice over whether we're subjected to applications such as facial recognition, emotion detection or risk-assessment tools. This will be the case when they're used by the state in the public sphere without our consent.

Regulating our future

The only way in which we can influence such deployments is through legislation, regulation and standards. There are already standards bodies that solicit opinion from the public, and many governments also have specialist committees that could be influenced. I believe that governments will need to regulate certain deployments through legislation, such as self-drive vehicles and facial recognition surveillance. We need to seek to influence, or even campaign for, appropriate legislation and regulation to protect our humanness. This will be controversial because, as I've already pointed out, there are powerful vested interests.

In the EU a potential ban on surveillance using facial recognition and other human attributes was mooted, but the eventual White Paper from the Commission watered this down.[12] No doubt powerful lobbying from vested interests was at work. However, as I mentioned earlier, some states in the USA have gone so far as to ban its use in public spaces.

Humans should retain responsibility for decision-making in areas where the lives of others are affected. For governments and corporations that means that we should not entrust to an algorithm the responsibility to make risk judgements about parole, reoffending, children potentially at risk, visa applications and many more areas.

Facial recognition should not be used as a determiner of identity, and biometric data generally should not be collected, stored and used without consent by the individual. This would mean banning facial recognition in all public places, just as in some cities in the USA have now done. Regrettably, in other countries, such as the UK, decisions have already been made by legislators or ethics bodies allowing the use of these applications in certain public spaces. The Federal Bureau of Investigation (FBI) in the USA has stated that in the next few years it sees facial recognition becoming a means of positive identification, rather than an investigative lead, overturning the status quo that positive identification, as we saw in chapter 7, is sometimes abused.[13]

As the AI Now Institute has suggested, legislation may also be required to restrict emotion detection algorithms being used in policing or interviewing.[14] In the area of autonomous vehicles, although we're a long way from this being practicable on public roads, there should be legislation that allows driver assistance: there should always be a human responsible for moral decisions.

---

12 European Commission, *White Paper on Artificial Intelligence*, p. 19.

13 C. Garvie, *Garbage in, Garbage Out: Face Recognition on Flawed Data*, Georgetown Law, Center on Privacy and Technology, 16 May 2019. The case is cited verbatim and is licensed under a Creative Commons Attribution 4.0 International licence, retrieved on 12 May 2010 from <https://www.flawedfacedata.com>.

14 L. Kelion, 'Emotion-Detecting Tech Should Be Restricted by Law – AI Now', *BBC News*, 12 December 2019, retrieved on 12 December 2019 from <https://www.bbc.co.uk/news/technology-50761116>.

It's my hope that the manifesto, together with the rationale set out in this book, will provide a useful guide for discussion, particularly around the potential harms to humans of certain AI applications. By pulling these together within a taxonomy of AI applications I hope that a sharper focus on the real issues confronting humanity may be possible. Enough consensus could also help to shape the thinking of wider society, influencing legislation, regulation and standards. This could serve to protect civilization, allowing us to be masters of AI technology rather than slaves to it.

The real challenge that we face as Christians isn't just how we avoid being sucked in by the allure of AI, but how to follow the true *Homo Deus*, who calls us to imitate him.

Following the true *Homo Deus*

If we're to be true followers of Christ, who is the only true God Man, we need to be constantly developing our relationship with him, to be in communion with God. We alone are responsible for our soul, to see that it's nourished and becoming more like Christ, rather than being diminished and slowly destroyed. I am not of course arguing that it's our efforts alone that bring about this change; rather, that God expects us to spend time with him, to cultivate spiritual disciplines that allow his Spirit to be at work within us to effect that change. As Paul put it, 'I can do all things through him who strengthens me' (Phil. 4:13).

Does our use of AI applications and other digital technology distract us from spending time alone with God in his Word and in prayer? Unfortunately, this technology when designed for personal use and convenience is fine-tuned to be seductive to engage and draw us in. This can steal away time that we could have spent with God, in his Word or in prayer – time that we need if we're to grow in grace and our knowledge of him. The nature of the battle is evident when we realize that it's in this time with God and his Word that we develop the discernment that we need in order to know the true mind of God: 'Do not be conformed to this world, but be transformed by the renewal of your mind, that by testing you may discern what is the will of God, what is good and acceptable and perfect' (Rom. 12:2).

The devil will use whatever tactics he can to steal that time from us, in order that we may have less discernment and unwittingly be seduced and drawn into this dangerous new digital world. This technology isn't neutral. Yes, it can be used for good, but we must be intentional, recognizing the dangers to our souls.

The great deception in play is that this technology frees us, makes our lives easier and more convenient; that it will ultimately save us and augment our humanity with something less flawed, something better than humanity alone. The acid test of whether we're being sucked into that deception is the state of our own souls. Are we really growing closer to God day by day, week by week, year by year? Are we, however falteringly, following Christ and imitating him, seeing our souls flourish as the fruit of the Spirit – a virtuous character – grows in us.

These are tough questions, with or without the enticement of the digital age and AI. Christians, since the birth of the church, have faced varying pressures, temptations and challenges to spiritual growth and behaviour. Our generation is experiencing perhaps the fastest pace of change and reshaping of civilization ever. We need, however, to be asking the same question that the early church asked when faced with cultural challenges to their faith – is this change right?

Let us stir each other up, encourage each other to a closer walk with Christ, who gave his all that we might be his. As we grapple with the issues set out in this book, it's my prayer that we'll be equipped to resist the devil and the diminishing of our true self as AI encroaches on our lives. It's also my prayer that as we confront the issues I've raised and respond accordingly, we may be salt and light in the communities in which God has placed us. May we – through our behaviour, lives and conversations – show a different way, and so be true icons of the God who made us.

With God's help we can be confident that, as we shine, we'll also act like salt, a preservative, for the future of our humanity.

Index of subjects

Index of Scripture references